A Parent's Guide to Eating Disorders

*Prevention and Treatment
of Anorexia Nervosa
and Bulimia*

BRETT VALETTE

Walker Publishing Co.   New York

To the families and individuals who have courageously struggled with an eating disorder and generously shared their experiences.

First published in the United States of America in 1988 by the Walker Publishing Company, Inc.

Published simultaneously in Canada by Thomas Allen & Son Canada, Limited, Markham, Ontario.

Library of Congress Cataloging-in-Publication Data

Valette, Brett Edouard.
A parent's guide to eating disorders.

Bibliography: p.
Includes index.
1. Eating disorders in children—Popular works.
2. Eating disorders in children—Patients—Family relationships.   I. Title.
RJ506.E18V35   1988   618.92′852   88-5521
ISBN 0-8027-1040-9

Printed in the United States of America

10 9 8 7 6 5 4 3 2 1

Text design by Manuela Paul

CONTENTS

FOREWORD

Eating disorders destructively affect the lives of hundreds of thousands of Americans. These pathologic and conflicted patterns of eating behavior are multidimensional, resulting in a diversity of disorders.

Brett Valette has written a comprehensive book that addresses all aspects of eating disorders. The author explains the origins and types of eating disorders, social and psychological factors, family dynamics, treatment, and stages of recovery. The case material and lack of technical jargon make the text both readable and accessible, and the author's sensitive exploration of the problems involved will help teens and adults cope with eating disorders as well as with their families. As Valette points out, eating problems very quickly become family problems.

With tragic results, our society has become narcissistically obsessed with body image, physical appearance, weight, size, and shape. Although there are no quick and easy solutions for any type of eating disorder, there are several techniques and steps that can lead to recovery. This book rationally explores the origins of and healthy alternatives to our collective preoccupation with weight.

With love, sensitivity, and solid clinical acumen, the author has written a book that will be extremely helpful for any person with an eating disorder or any person living with someone who has an eating disorder. Pass it on to a friend!

GARY G. FORREST, ED.D., PH.D.

Clinical Psychologist and Executive Director
Psychotherapy Associates, P.C., and The Institute For Addictive
Behavioral Change,
Colorado Springs, Colorado.

ACKNOWLEDGMENTS

I wish to thank Dr. Dorothy Guerin for her knowledge and skill in helping me prepare the manuscript; Kim Welch, R.D., for her assistance with dietary questions; and Ingrid Justin, M.D., for consultation regarding medical issues. I would also like to thank my parents, Ed and Marilyn Valette, for their love and encouragement; my sisters, Colette and Julet, who have taught me so much about living, loving, and laughing; my friend Lita Van Wagenen, who has always believed in me; John Sackett, who trusted me and enthusiastically supported the writing of this book; and especially Raymond Farrow, for introducing me to the field of psychotherapy. Finally, a special thank you to Dr. Robert Schuller, whose principles and inspiration helped me believe in myself and, in turn, help others believe in themselves.

INTRODUCTION

Pam had the look all fashion-savvy fifth-graders crave. She was slim and vivacious. Her blond hair was expensively styled and her little earrings were real gold. From her red knit shirt to her white leather Reeboks, she could have stepped into my office right out of the pages of *Young Miss*.

Pam's parents, successful horse breeders, brought her in to see me about a year ago. They were at the end of their wits, they said. For the last two years, this beautiful girl had been quietly getting up from the table after nearly every meal, excusing herself, and going into the bathroom to vomit. Apparently she had no control over her vomiting, and not one of the pediatricians and internists they had taken her to could discover what was wrong with her. When her doctors began to suspect an emotional problem, they referred her to me.

At first glance, Pam's emotional state seemed as impeccable as her grooming. She seemed satisfied with her weight and her appearance. She had lots of friends, got very good grades, and appeared comfortable with her family. No wonder her parents were confused and distraught. They didn't have a clue to what was going on. They were torn between concern for a well-loved child and anger over the way she was wrecking their family life for no apparent reason. They were beginning to think Pam was vomiting on purpose, to get attention.

What impressed me most about Susan was her adultlike poise. Even in a rumpled hospital bed, so emaciated that her shoulder blades under blue satin pajamas poked out like small angel wings, she had the composure of a successful politician.

Successful is just what Susan had always been, at everything she ever tried. Her teachers all liked her. (What teacher can resist a child who talks like an adult?) She spoke Spanish and French fluently. She was a promising ballerina.

But the crowning achievement of Susan's young life was starving herself down to 80 pounds in just ten months—the point at which her frightened parents had her admitted to the hospital. "It's like she thinks food will poison her," her mother said.

For weeks Susan had been eating barely enough to keep her alive. Orange juice and a tiny piece of toast for breakfast, no lunch, no snacks. At dinnertime she would cut up her food in bird-size bits, push it around on her plate, and hope her family wouldn't notice how little of it went into her mouth.

What they did notice, when she could no longer hide the fact under three layers of clothes, was that Susan was losing weight at a disturbing rate—two or three pounds a week. Her doctor and the hospital staff were now monitoring her diet carefully. And Susan was as polite and agreeable as usual. But after a week in the hospital, she continued to lose weight.

Unlike most of my patients, Becky came in to see me on her own. She said she needed to talk to someone. It was her first year in college and the first time she had ever been away from home, which was about two thousand miles away.

Becky had a hard time getting her story out. For one thing, she was gasping for breath—she had run the seven miles from campus—but she was also fighting back tears. Its seems that her freshman year at college was turning out to be a mixed bag. The social life was great—a "good" sorority, lots of dates and parties—and she stood an excellent chance of making the women's running team. She had nice friends and decent grades. And she was absolutely miserable.

The problem was (here the tears finally spilled over), she was terrified of becoming fat. So terrified that she was taking about seventy laxatives a week to rush food out of her system before it could turn into those hated pounds. She had been doing it for over a year now, secretly. She told me she didn't want any of her friends to know "because it's just too gross," but that she had tried and failed again and again to tell her parents. "It's not their fault," she said. "It's me. I guess I'm just afraid of what they'll think of me."

Becky fought her war against fat not only with laxatives but with nonstop physical activity, including running, aerobic dancing, and workouts in the college gym. She got up at 5:00 A.M. to get in an hour and a half of running before class. Sometimes she ran in place while she studied. It became very important for her to keep running; otherwise, the enemy would catch up with her.

Jeff was so proud to make the wrestling team in his first year of high school that he didn't object when his coach told him he needed to lose ten pounds before his first match, which was only a week away. Jeff had never tried to control his weight before, but his teammates told him how to do it: fast for two or three days, then, when the hunger became intolerable, binge and throw up.

During this week of fasting and bingeing, Jeff suffered from headaches and dizziness but he said nothing. He was afraid the coach would kick him off the team if he complained. And he felt sure his parents would put a stop to his weight-loss measures if they knew how drastic they were. A year later, Jeff is still fasting, bingeing, and throwing up. Now he does it all the time, not just before matches.

Pam, Susan, Becky, and Jeff are all good kids by anybody's standards—conscientious, hard working, and disciplined. They are also lucky in many ways: They are attractive and talented, their families care about them and have enough money to provide for all their needs. But all four suffer from either bulimia nervosa or anorexia nervosa, serious eating disorders that are wrecking the health and happiness of an alarming number of young people in our country today.

How many? The American Psychiatric Association's *Diagnostic and Statistical Manual* estimates that one percent of our teenagers suffer from an eating disorder[1]—a conservative figure that does not include preteens and those who do not display all the symptoms listed in the *Manual*. A recent study at Stanford University showed that thirteen percent of the 1,728 tenth-graders surveyed showed one or more characteristics of bulimia.[2]

Most diagnosed cases occur in people between the ages of 14 and 25. The average age of the teenagers among the 400 or so cases I have treated was 16. In addition, a growing number of children between 8 and 15 are falling victim to anorexia and bulimia. An estimated one in twenty of these children is male, and their number seems to be increasing. Because the majority of sufferers are female, I will generally refer to them with the feminine pronoun throughout the book. But my remarks apply to boys as well as girls.

Those who suffer from anorexia and bulimia develop a range of symptoms that are described in Appendix 1. Briefly, anorexia nervosa (usually shortened to *anorexia*) is an intense fear of becoming fat, accompanied by self-starvation and refusal to gain weight, which results in a loss of fifteen percent or more of the original body weight. Bulimia nervosa (usually shortened to *bulimia*) is less easy to recognize because sufferers generally maintain a normal body weight. However, as many as fifty percent of anorexics develop bulimia. In these cases, the alternating binges and fasts result in noticeable weight fluctuation. Bulimia is characterized by repeated episodes of rapidly eating a large amount of food, usually in less than two hours, followed by self-induced vomiting, excessive exercise, or use of laxatives or diuretics. This book's main concern is to explore the complex thoughts and feelings that accompany the physical symptoms of anorexia and bulimia.

This book also concentrates on eating disorders in children and teenagers who are still living at home. I believe that you, the parents, are not only strong allies in helping your child recover from an eating disorder—you can help *prevent* eating disorders.

That means challenging some current myths about eating disorders.

Myth #1: Only emotionally unbalanced children get
eating disorders.
Fact: Every child growing up today is at risk.

Children growing up in our current society are pressured to do more, feel more, and see more than they are prepared to handle. From the time they can focus their eyes on a television screen, they are bombarded with messages telling them to grow up—fast. Be sexy! Be successful! Get rich! They learn that to become rich and successful they must go to a good college and find a high-paying job. To do that, they must get high grades in school or, they imagine, they are doomed to lifelong failure. There is little room at the top for average kids or those who don't conform to their school's developmental timetable. Late bloomers run the risk of being put into a special class for slow learners or, in high school, being shifted from the academic track to more vocational-oriented education.

What's more, it's not enough to be bright and accomplished. Young people learn early that to be successful they have to look successful. That means not just having the right clothes, accessories, and hairstyle, but the right kind of body—a thin body, no matter what it takes.

Add to these pressures the easy availability of drugs and the inducements to try sex at an early age, and it is no wonder our youngsters are confused and anxious. The child who develops an eating disorder isn't defective or crazy. She is struggling with the same pressures that all of us, but especially young people, are trying to handle.

There's no escape, no island left where we can raise our children untouched by drugs, diet pill advertisements, and achievement tests. But we can try to understand the overwhelming demands our children face. We can recognize that some of these demands cause more unhappiness than they are worth and that some are downright insane. And we can fight back. In chapter 1, we will look at some of the social pressures that contribute to our eating disorders epidemic. In the chapters that follow, I'll suggest some ways to help your child handle these pressures.

> *Myth #2:* Dieting is perfectly normal these days. No need to be concerned about a child who diets to be thinner.
> *Fact:* Dieting is one of the early warning signs of a potential eating disorder.

A study done at Wellesley College showed that over half of our young girls from 10 to 15 may already be dieting or want to diet.[3] A more recent University of California study of fourth-grade girls in San Francisco showed that 80 percent are dieting or want to diet.[4] That means these 9-year-olds are swapping diet books, counting the number of calories in a popsicle, and comparing notes on how much weight they lost. These are among the earliest symptoms reported by my patients.

Does that mean every kid who diets will develop an eating disorder? Of course not. The causes of anorexia and bulimia are many and very complex. But one thing is clear—a trim, active, healthy youngster who is seriously worried about being overweight is already out of touch with her own body. She is risking health, pleasure, and self-esteem for the sake of a phony ideal—an ideal that is lining the pockets of powerful interest groups in this country. That, it seems to me, is reason enough for concern.

It's not the only reason. Nobody ever woke up on a Monday morning and discovered she had bulimia or anorexia nervosa. Eating disorders develop by stages over a period of months, even years. Though no two people ever react in exactly the same way, my own research leads me to believe that every sufferer goes through stages that are clear enough to recognize if you know the warning signs, which are discussed in chapters 2, 3, and 4. For now, I will say only that it is easier to prevent an eating disorder than cure it, and it is easier to treat one in its beginning stages.

Myth #3: The obsessive pursuit of slenderness is discouraged among males in our society.
Fact: Males share with girls and women the pressures
that may lead to drastic weight control.

Most males who develop eating disorders have a strong motive
for being concerned with body size and weight. Many are involved
in sports with a strict weight requirement. To a wrestler, vomiting
and using laxatives and diuretics may seem the ideal way to achieve
quick weight loss before a match. Some male runners use extreme
measures to increase their speed by reducing their body fat to
dangerous levels—in some cases as low as three percent of their
body weight. Body builders may become so preoccupied with body
image that weight control takes priority over health. Because males
who develop eating disorders are even more secretive than women
about their condition, their number is difficult to estimate, but it is
generally thought to be increasing.

Myth #4: Parents are to blame for their children's
eating disorder.
Fact: The parents of most young patients are conscientious and caring. The causes of an eating disorder are
too complex to pin the blame on anyone.

Typically, parents feel guilty or ashamed when their child
develops an eating disorder. They wonder if they have been too
strict, too lenient, or too protective. Many of the articles in the
popular press may reinforce parents' guilt by suggesting that they
have done something terrible to damage their child. They may also
give the impression that only a specially trained professional can
do anything to help the child recover.

That's what this book is all about—to give you, the parent, a
clearer idea of how an eating disorder develops in a young child or
teenager, and to suggest what you can do to promote a healthy
change. My objective isn't to tell you what to do in order to be a
good parent. You already know that. You know you need to be

supportive, listen to your child, communicate openly, and resolve conflicts so nobody comes out a loser. I'm firmly convinced that most parents have the desire to do all these things and to do them well. What they don't always have is the specific knowledge of how to do them.

Chapters 5 and 7 provide examples of how families can cope with and resolve the problem of an eating disorder. In chapters 7 and 9, specific techniques are explored for getting a withdrawn child to open up and for confronting a hostile child without creating a power struggle.

I believe parents have the power to help their child along the road to recovery from an eating disorder. My goal is to help you find the knowledge and self-reliance you need to use your power well.

Notes

1. *Diagnostic and Statistical Manual of Mental Disorders*, 3rd ed., rev. (Washington, DC: American Psychiatric Association, 1987).

2. J. D. Killen et al., "Self-induced Vomiting and Laxative and Diuretic Use Among Teenagers," *The Journal of the American Medical Association* 255, no. 11 (March 21, 1986): 1447–49.

3. Pamela Erens, "Bodily Harm: Help for Women Trapped in the Binge-Purge Cycle," *Ms.* 14, no. 4 (October 1985): 82.

4. "Fourth-Grade Girls These Days Ponder Weighty Matters," *The Wall Street Journal*, February 11, 1986, 1.

CHAPTER 1

THIN AT ANY COST:

How Our National Obsession Affects Young Children and Teenagers

I can't stand the thought of being fat. It's just so ugly. If I ever got really fat, I know what I'd do. I'd go off to my favorite spot, a pretty place by a lake I know, and die.

Sandy, 14

Each generation has its own idea about what a perfect body should look like. Thirty years ago, that body was full and rounded and belonged to Marilyn Monroe. Today's ideal body is lean and taut and belongs to Jane Fonda. But a more important change has taken place during the last thirty years.

Back in those days, most of the general public were content to admire Marilyn Monroe's beautiful face and figure. They did not rush out and collectively buy millions of dollars worth of books, records, and rowing machines in hopes of transforming themselves into her. It is only in the last twenty years or so that a majority of us have come to think we have to starve and sweat ourselves into the shape of our favorite media stars and models.

We're starving and sweating on a grand scale, too. More than

1

twenty million Americans claim to be on some kind of diet to lose weight. We are pouring billions annually into the weight-loss industry. And, to judge from a recent survey, we have created a national phobia of obesity that ranks right up there with our fears of death and aging. Of a recently polled group of Americans— facing threats of war, international terrorism, and economic disaster—nearly 40 percent claimed that their greatest fear was "getting fat."

This is the climate our kids are growing up in. They can't remember how it was way back when most of the public hardly gave their weight a thought—when people generally ate what tasted good and bought clothes that would conceal the results as becomingly as possible.

To our children, such a let-it-be attitude about body weight would seem almost indecent. It's easy to see why. From the time they were out of diapers, these youngsters have been learning our society's eleventh commandment: Thou shalt diet and be thin. They have seen and heard it on television and in the movies, gathered it from magazines, picked it up from the other kids at school. They've overheard their families predict that cousin Elsie won't find a husband if she doesn't lose 20 pounds. They may even have noticed that the all-American kid costume—blue jeans—is designed to look good only on slim bodies.

It's hard enough for an adult to ignore this kind of nonstop propaganda. For a youngster in her early teens or pre-teens, it's next to impossible to ignore. She's still groping for an identity and is self-conscious about her changing body. She wants to fit in at school, and appear attractive to boys. "Thou shalt diet and be thin" looks like an easy formula for achieving all her heart's desires— beauty, popularity, love, and success.

Maybe she'll decide that skipping breakfast every day or skimping on lunch is a small price to pay for looking slender and fashionable, like the magazine models. Or maybe she'll clip a low-calorie diet from a magazine and try it out for a week or two. If she is like most young girls, her pursuit of the impossible dream won't go much beyond this point. The highest price she will pay is substandard nutrition.

But for others, and their number is growing, the price may be much higher. Either way, you can help your children by being aware of the pressures our society exerts to be thin at any cost.

These Messages from Our Sponsors

The two little girls are like exotic flowers, slender and strikingly beautiful. Their eyes sparkle as they chat excitedly in perfect Parisian French. What can they be discussing with such animation? According to the subtitles on the television screen, they are saying they can hardly wait to grow up so they can use a certain brand of diet pill, just like their mother.

What message does this widely aired television advertisement convey? It's saying that certain old-world arbiters of taste and culture, like the French, see diet pills as a natural part of the good life. It's also saying that diet pills are a natural part of growing up—an exciting event that these young girls look forward to as ecstatically as to their first kiss.

We have had diet product advertisements with us for some time, but this is a new wrinkle. This one is trying to convince us that dieting is not just for weight-conscious career women and home-makers, it's something little girls should be seriously thinking about. In another diet-product commercial, the words are more direct, though the visual message is not as powerful. An attractive adult model tells us she has been dieting since she was 14, but could never lose an ounce until she tried the brand of pill she is now hawking.

"Oh, nobody takes stuff on television that seriously," you may be thinking. But psychologists who study the effects of television on children's learning do not agree. Television is the most powerful communication medium in our whole visually oriented society. The words in some of the commercials and shows may be so silly that even your youngest kids make fun of them. But the words on television don't really count very much. While youngsters are giggling at the words, their minds are being shaped by the hypnotic power of the pictures. Teenagers of today have typically watched 15,000 or more hours of television during their lifetime. And there is no longer any doubt that the messages they receive influence their beliefs and behavior.

Thin is Where the Action is

The leading characters in our current crop of television shows come in one size—slender. The few characters who do carry a few extra pounds are likely to be elderly, matronly, in low-status occupations, or on the wrong side of the law. The message is clear and consistent: men and women who are involved and successful in today's society are young or young-looking and thin.

While it is true that young people can look around and see that successful people in the real world come in a variety of sizes and shapes, psychologists have shown that television images have a unique power to mold children's attitudes. When a certain group, like thin people, shows up frequently on the television screen, children assume that group must play an important role in society. If a group rarely appears, children assume they are not important. Children's attitudes are also affected by how respectfully a group is portrayed in the television shows and advertisements. If heavy people are regularly shown in low-class or low-comedy roles, young viewers will learn to look down on them.[1] It doesn't take kids long to figure out what our culture expects of them: To be successful, diet and be thin.

But what we see on television is a special kind of thin. Most of us could starve ourselves down to slivers and still not look anything like those sleek bodies that flit across our screen day and night. The bodies we see on our network television shows and commercials are those of elite dancers, athletes, and models—men and women who make a full-time job of keeping themselves in show-room condition. Male or female, these bodies are young, strong, and built for action, whether it's lunging after a volleyball on a beach or striding into a boardroom. The faces of the women and men are often surgically fixed and usually made up to a state of perfection never seen on this side of the television screen.

The characters portrayed lead lives to match. Socially, they are polished and at ease. They have many friends and lovers, exciting jobs, lots of money, and wonderful clothes and cars. What goes on in the hearts and minds of these characters? No one knows or cares. All we see are their social power, their clothes, and their figures. Most of all, their figures.

It Just Takes a Little Willpower

Sure, this is only show business, but the constant parade of perfect bodies affects all of us to some extent. It can deeply influence the lives of children and young teens. These marvelous-looking men and women can fill one of young people's most important needs—a positive goal to strive for in their search for fulfillment.

Physical perfection is a goal few will achieve. The right kind of face is a gift of heredity; the right kinds of clothes cost more than many of us can afford. We don't all have what it takes to be the ultimate social success or to earn a six-figure income. Some of us couldn't get a volleyball across a net if our lives depended on it. But, as the message goes, anybody with a grain of character and commitment can control her body size and achieve at least that much of the ideal. Maybe we can't all afford designer clothes, but we can eat less, eat low-cal desserts, drink diet soda, take diet pills, and get thinner. Much, much thinner. But achieving the flawless body of a television star is a hopelessly unrealistic goal. The fact is, we don't have that much control over the shape of our bodies. Some of us are broader and bigger-boned than others, and no amount of dieting and aerobics can change that. Physiologists are finding that we are all born with a certain unchangeable number of fat cells. There is also a lot of individual variation in the rate at which we burn calories: some of us can gain weight on 1,200 calories a day, some on 5,000.

Another point young girls may overlook in their desire to look like a "Dallas" star is that women naturally have more fat on their bodies than men. That image of lean, lithe perfection on television is impossible for most women and men to achieve, no matter how hard they try.

The Addictive Cycle

Striving for such an unrealistic goal can cripple children's emotional growth. It can make them belittle their own abilities and despise their own appearance, no matter how attractive they are. They may ignore real ways to gain self-acceptance—seeking new friends, developing their talents—in search of a hopeless ideal that leaves them feeling blue and empty. They may then fall victim to a kind of emotional misery that is so common in our society that it often passes for normal behavior. It's called the *addictive cycle*.

This is how the addictive cycle works. Let's suppose I feel my life isn't as happy and fulfilled as I'd like it to be. Trained as we all are to seek consumer solutions to our personal problems, I immediately think that I might feel less lousy if I bought something, maybe a new car. I also consider changing my appearance in some way. Some new clothes? A new diet so I'll look better in them? It's true that we feel better and more accepted when we improve our appearance or wear nice clothes. But the confidence we gain by changing our looks or buying new things seldom lasts long. It can't, for the new clothes or new diet only detour us around the real-life problems that keep us from feeling genuinely happy.

What a disappointment when those high expectations don't pan out. After spending a bundle or mustering the willpower to lose 5 or 10 pounds, we find that we not only gain the weight back—as 90 percent of dieters do—but we feel more blue and dissatisfied than ever. When the short-term fix quickly fades, leaving us as unhappy as we were when we started, the typical solution is to buy more clothes, lose more weight, maybe even get cosmetic surgery. But such external solutions to internal problems simply don't work. We need internal solutions to internal problems.

First, we need to examine our feelings to find the source of the problem. Do we need to develop a better self-image? Do we need to become more confident or less critical of ourselves? Do we need to work on our personal relationships? If I have a troubled marriage, buying a new Volvo won't fix it. If I do not like myself, losing 5, 10, or 50 pounds won't change those negative feelings. The addictive cycle keeps repeating itself until we take action and move toward emotional growth.

The process just described gets millions hooked on dieting—trying and failing again and again to achieve a Madison Avenue body. Like a powerful drug, dieting holds out a promise of happiness it can't keep. Worst of all, children brought up in an environment of consumer solutions to unhappiness can easily fall into this same addictive trap.

You're Not Quite Good Enough

The magazine at the checkout stand features a luscious-looking three-layer chocolate cake on its cover. Slightly to the left of this mouth-watering treat is the cover line, "Stay Slim for Keeps: New Doctor's Plan Shows You How."

Is somebody confused here? Isn't it self-defeating to promote a diet plan alongside this 4,000-calorie dessert? Not at all. The people who designed that split-personality cover knew exactly what they were doing. They are ensuring that even while you sink your fork into that sensuous fudge icing, you will feel guilty enough to resolve to start this new diet tomorrow. The main message of all the women's and teens' magazines is clear and simple: You should think about your weight and appearance at all times. The way you are is not quite good enough.

Do you have dry skin? Blemishes? Cellulite? More than an inch of pinch? An uncoordinated wardrobe? Of course you do. So does nearly everyone. But—so the message goes—defects like these are obstacles to a happy life. They hide the "real" person and ruin her confidence.

It's hard enough for the worldly wise adult magazine reader to shrug off this message. Young teens, already self-conscious about their appearance, are extremely vulnerable. Nearly every page shouts, "The way you are is not good enough!"

Here's a picture of a woman grieving over the brown spots on her hands. "I'm so ashamed," she's murmuring. A hair-color advertisement promises to cover up "ugly gray" and let the "natural you" shine through. A diet center invites readers to "Open the door to a slim new you!" An article on *liposuction* (the surgical removal of fat by a vacuum process) suggests that imperfect thighs should make the reader despise herself enough to suffer the pain and expense of major surgery.

In fact, most women and young girls are not completely satisfied with the way they look. ("You all aren't any good just the way you are—are you?" Television talk-show host Phil Donahue recently challenged his mostly female audience as he opened discussion on the day's topic, the cosmetics industry. There were a few uncomfortable titters.) In particular, the majority of women and girls are unhappy with their weight. According to a 1983 *Glamour* survey of 33,000 women, three-fourths thought they weighed too much. About the same percentage of fourth-grade girls recently surveyed in Chicago and San Francisco thought they were overweight. Various studies of young high-school women indicate that nearly 60 percent think they're too fat.[2]

With mass insecurities like these to feed on, advertisements and articles that promise a new and beautiful you are bound to have a steady supply of readers. And so, the same airbrushed faces and slender bodies show up month after month in the magazines—

along with the promise that anyone can look the same if they diet, exercise, and buy the products advertised. It is an invitation to jump into the addictive trap, to look for happiness in a place where it can never be found.

You Want To Be Healthy, Don't You?

We Americans have retained enough of the old Puritan spirit to be uncomfortable spending vast amounts of time and money on our looks. Men and women over 40 can remember a parent criticizing their vanity and saying things like "beauty is only skin deep" if they got too deeply engrossed in their appearance. Even today, some people complain that narcissists are overrunning the country. That is why the merchants of pefection stress looking wonderful less than they do feeling wonderful. These manufacturers are appealing to health and fitness instead of pure vanity.

Being thin is good for you, they're saying. Being fat can cause high blood pressure, high blood cholesterol, diabetes, and certain kinds of cancer, not to mention the psychological suffering that goes along with being "oversized" in our society. They often quote the National Institutes of Health (NIH) panel as saying that obesity is a "killer" disease.[3]

From the marketing standpoint, the weight-loss industry's use of this famous medical report has been very successful. It has boosted the sale not only of diet aids but of aerobics shoes and Spandex tights. From the standpoint of logic, it deserves a closer look.

Most doctors today do agree with the NIH panel's opinion that anyone who weighs 20 percent or more over the Metropolitan Insurance Company's 1983 Height and Weight Table is risking untimely death, especially if heart disease runs in the family. But research has not resolved this issue entirely and this medical opinion is not unanimous by any means. In fact, many prominent doctors flatly disagree.

Neurobiologist Paul Ernsberger at Cornell University, for example, points to the widely publicized Framingham Heart Study, in which the heaviest women proved to have a lower death rate than those who were at the "desirable" insurance table weights. Ernsberger claims that "Fatness is *not* associated with a higher death rate. In fact, in every given population examined, the thinnest people have the highest death rate."[4] Other researchers, like cardiovascular specialist Ancel Keys of the University of Minnesota and gerontologist Reubin Andres of Johns Hopkins, disagree with the NIH panel's view that a weight of even five or ten percent over the "ideal" poses an increased risk of heart disease. Their studies indicate that in the absence of high blood pressure a few extra pounds may even be an aid to good health.[5]

But suppose the widespread belief that fat poses a serious health risk were proven beyond a doubt. The fact is that our national obsession with thin bodies springs from a deeper source than concern for our health. The fashion and teen magazines are targeted at the young and the weight conscious. But survey after survey shows that the majority of these weight-conscious young women aren't overweight at all.

A study of women at Cornell University, for example, showed that of the 48 percent who said they were too fat, only 5 percent were actually over "ideal" insurance table weights. According to studies at other colleges, nearly 35 percent of women undergraduates are actually underweight, but only 5 percent acknowledge it.[6]

If health and fitness were the main motives for our national fat phobia, would 50,000 Americans, mostly women, every year risk having their stomachs partly stitched up so they will feel full on a small amount of food? Or having their jaws wired together to prevent them from ingesting much of anything except liquids? Or enduring intestinal bypass surgery? In this operation, a large portion of the intestines is closed off, limiting the amount of food that can be comfortably eaten and also the amount of nutrients that can be absorbed. Would they have put up with the dangers and discomforts of "starch blockers" before the FDA banned them? Or any of the other weight-control gimmicks that keep cropping up?

It is possible, in fact, that some of the problems associated with fatness may be caused by the very things many weight-conscious Americans are doing to get thin. We know that the familiar "yo-yo" process of rapid weight loss and gain contributes to high blood pressure. Liquid protein diets have caused not only heart trouble but sudden death. The ingredients in many diet pills have been linked with side effects ranging from heart seizures to psychoses. It's a profitable business, yes. Healthy? No.

Fitness Equals Sex

Take a close look at the pages of any of the popular teen and fashion magazines and you will read a strangely mixed message. On the one hand, many of the magazines emphasize health and contain much medically sound advice. In article after article, readers are advised to see a doctor before starting a diet and to avoid fads and extremes. They are urged to eat a balanced diet and not lose more than a pound a week. Famous psychologists tell readers to accept themselves as they are and not to base their self-esteem on their body size.

But, like Mom's good advice about always dressing warmly and eating a good breakfast, these sensible messages get drowned out by more seductive ones. Like advertisements for diet plans that promise you will lose 12 pounds in twenty-one days, or the one that promises you will drop a dangerous 8 pounds a week ("Designed for you—the young and lovable teen"). These are followed by page after full-color page of slender, expensively dressed models. The unspoken message is always the same: "Look perfect, spend money, be sexy."

A few years ago, *Vogue* started a small uproar by showing a nude woman hoisting two grocery sacks to illustrate an article on fitness. Now nude models in erotic poses are a common sight in the fashion magazines, and they are often promoting a health or fitness product.

This double message is especially obvious in *Shape*, a special favorite of many of my young patients. ("Strength is Sexy," blared the cover line on a recent issue.) The articles are about body building and good nutrition. An advisory board of distinguished health professionals leads us to believe that the information is accurate and up-to-date. Fitness is the key word, but the seductive, nearly nude models in the shoe and dancewear advertisements are selling sex.

Health and fitness are not the real motives behind our society's mania for thinness and our children know it. They hear the real message many times a day, every day of their lives: Look perfect, spend money, be sexy. The way you are is not good enough.

The Folklore of Fat

> When I was in third grade we got a new boy named Carl in our class. He must have weighed about 150 pounds, and he just grossed everybody out. We never made fun of him, and I always tried to be nice to him. But he never had any good friends. It was sad. Of course it was really his own fault he looked like that. *Denise, 15*

Any of us who don't conform to the commandment to diet and be thin will pay some sort of price. For young people, the price can be exorbitant—ridicule, social exclusion, even bullying. No matter what talents or personal qualities they may have, they quickly learn that their weight makes them unacceptable.

It's not the extra pounds, per se, that cause the rejection. The problem is that our culture attaches all sorts of values to body shape. Our children learn very early that any deviation from the socially approved shape can expose a person to discrimination. For some reason, obesity is the most dreaded deviation of all.

The idea that our body shape determines what kind of person we are has existed for a long time. During the early 1940s, the psychologist William Sheldon claimed that there are three body types and that our predominant type determines our personality, our character, even our intelligence. The three major types he described were the *ectomorph* (a long, thin, narrow body), the *mesomorph* (a muscular, athletic body), and the *endormorph* (a rounded, fleshy, slow-moving body).[7]

Few psychologists today take Sheldon's ideas seriously. His methods of investigation were unscientific, and his theory is inconsistent with what we have since learned about human personality. However, as a society we act as though these ideas were true. We have learned to idealize Sheldon's mesomorphic body build and associate positive character traits with it, such as bravery, energy, and assertiveness. Concurrently, we associate negative character traits with the round, fleshy endomorphs. This folklore of fat is so deeply ingrained in our minds that our children pick it up as toddlers. By the time they have entered school, they accept it without question. Many studies among school-age youngsters show this to be the case.

Nobody Loves a Fat Rag Doll

Researchers have found, for example, that both children and adults make very harsh judgments about people with rounded body builds, believing them to be lazy, stupid, ugly, mean, and dirty. It is usually assumed that they are sad and lonely. No wonder. On the other hand, those blessed with an athletic mesomorphic body are judged as brave, strong, and friendly.[8]

Most fat people, research shows, suffer from this harsh stereotyping. Few, if any, have a good word to say for fat children. Obesity is generally regarded as a full-fledged disability—one that research subjects consider less attractive than missing body parts or facial deformities. Ideas like these make no sense, of course. Like any other kind of folklore, they spring from a deep, little-understood place in our minds.

Even the preschool children researchers worked with had fully developed fat phobias. In one well-known study, preschoolers were presented with two life-sized rag dolls that looked alike except that one was fat and the other was thin. Of the children who had a preference, 91 percent preferred the thin doll. Further study showed that this age group liked thin children even better than children of average weight. We have good reason to believe that kids learn to idealize a thin figure even before they learn to read.

There is no question that these negative judgments about fat have deep consequences for youngsters. Those who are over the idealized weight will have to put up with some degree of rejection. Both boys and girls are uncomfortable with heavy children and tend to keep their distance. What goes on inside a child who sees that her body is unacceptable to those around her? Many of these children find it too painful to accept the idea that they are inferior to others, so they simply deny that they are fat. In their imaginations, they see themselves as looking like everyone else. In playing this game, they spare themselves bad feelings, but lose touch with their own bodies. And without a clear sense of their own bodies, it will be almost impossible for them to develop a strong self-image and positive self-esteem.

By the time they have reached their early teens, youngsters feel the pressure to conform most strongly. By then, girls have deeply internalized the belief that fat is not beautiful, and that beauty means approval in the eyes of males. Young boys feel a need to appear fit and strong, to be good in sports, and to be admired by both girls and boys. Few young teens feel secure enough to risk rejection by their schoolmates.

So there is little choice. If children are overweight, whether a little or a lot, they have the option of getting thin or living with daily humiliation. If they are of average weight or thin, they will feel they have to avoid gaining weight, whatever the cost. Avoiding or shedding pounds can become the number-one priority with these youngsters, and at an alarmingly early age.

Thin Rhymes with Win

The motive for active children and teens to diet and watch their weight isn't always their concern for appearance, though. In many cases, it starts when they get involved in school sports or ballet lessons. Stories like Buddy's, for example, are common:

> When I was in tenth grade, the wrestling coach used to get on my case about my weight all the time—he wanted me to drop 7 or 8 pounds. Some of the other guys did really weird things, like sit by the radiator in class so they'd sweat a lot. Or keep spitting into a paper cup to get some of the water out of their system. I just didn't eat anything for about two days before we weighed in. Then after the match I'd eat up everything in the kitchen.

School sports are serious business. Kids who participate are under strong pressure from coaches and teammates to improve their performance. The problem is that reducing body weight is the first thing most trainers think about when trying to improve an athlete's speed and endurance. This is especially true in the case of wrestlers, gymnasts, distance runners, and body builders.

A teenager needs more calories than an adult. Her hearty appetite, and in some cases her natural body build, makes it hard if not impossible for her to get her weight to the desired level. So she may learn from more experienced athletes, occasionally even from coaches and teachers, extreme and unhealthful ways to lose weight. Bingeing and purging are all too common among teenaged athletes. So are fasting and the use of caffeine, diuretics, laxatives, and diet pills. These unhealthful habits then get reinforced when the young athlete is praised for losing weight.

Young women who pursue sports and dance are often under greater pressure than male athletes. As we have seen, young women in our society tend to think they are too fat regardless of what they weigh—they don't always need a teammate or teacher to tell them so. Although like boys, their main interest is in performing well, girls who reduce their body weight to the desired level often suffer other bad effects besides the damage caused by bizarre eating habits.

Ballerinas, gymnasts, and distance runners typically have less than 10 percent of their body weight as fat, occasionally as little as

5 percent. However, it is normal for teenage girls to have anywhere from 20 to 25 percent of their body weight as fat, compared with 14 percent for boys. When a young woman reduces her body fat to the low level demanded in dance and certain sports, she can set off a chain of dangerous consequences. Doctors who have researched young girls studying ballet have found that girls who diet and exercise to keep a ballerina's tiny figure often start menstruating much later than average. This delay in normal sexual development causes a delay in bone development, which means these youngsters are in danger of developing curvature of the spine, brittle bones, and stress fractures.[9]

But after a lifetime of brainwashing by the media, thorough grounding in the folklore of fat, and praise by adults for losing weight, young children and teens will find it hard to believe that getting thin may not be in their best interest. The pressures are overwhelming—too great for them to deal with alone.

Notes

1. This research is summarized in Joyce N. Sprafkin and Robert M. Liebert, "Sex-typing and Children's Television Preferences," in *Heart and Home: Images of Women in the Mass Media* (New York: Oxford University Press, 1978).

2. Summarized by Michael Levine in *Kenyon College Alumni Bulletin*, Winter 1985.

3. The National Institutes of Health, "The Search for Health," (Bethesda, MD: NIH, 1985). Supt. of Docs no. HE 20, 3038: 062. (Summary of report in leaflet form.)

4. Carol Sternhill, "We'll Always Be Fat but Fat Can Be Fit," *Ms.* 13, no. 11 (May 1985): 144.

5. Kim Chernin, *The Obsession: Reflections on the Tyranny of Slenderness*, (New York: Harper & Row, 1981), 31.

6. Katherine Halmi et al., "Binge Eating and Vomiting: A Survey of a College Population," *Psychological Medicine* 11 (1981): 697–706.

7. William H. Sheldon, *The Varieties of Temperament: A Psychology of Constitutional Differences* (New York: Harper and Brothers, 1942).

8. For a summary of the research mentioned in this section, see Sue Dyren-

forth, Orland Wooley, and Susan Wooley, "A Woman's Body in a Man's World: A Review of Findings on Body Image and Weight Control," in Jane Kaplan, ed., *A Woman's Conflict* (Englewood Cliffs, NJ: Prentice-Hall Press, 1980).

9. Michelle Warren et al., "Scoliosis and Fractures in Young Ballet Dancers," *New England Journal of Medicine* 314, no. 21 (May 22, 1986): 1348–53.

CHAPTER 2

TUNING IN AND TALKING BACK:

Prevention

My mom and dad were always on some kind of diet. They always measured food like tunafish, cottage cheese, and peanut butter. In a way it drove me crazy, but I thought it was what everybody did. I felt like I should be measuring food, too.

Allison, 17

What causes eating disorders? We don't know exactly. We know the diet industry creates the ideal climate for them, and that the social and biological pressures of adolescence often trigger eating disorders. We are sure that family communication patterns and family attitudes toward food and fat are important factors. And we suspect that body chemistry may play a part in some cases. But much more research needs to be done before we will know what causes young people to put themselves through the misery of anorexia and bulimia. Usually, what we call the cause—a major disappointment or rejection—is really the last straw. The trouble may have been brewing quietly for years.

Two things seem clear, though, from my own experience in talking with these youngsters and their parents. One is that eating disorders have more to do with feelings than with food. In a full-blown eating disorder, food is nothing more than a way to communicate feelings when there seems to be no other way to express them. Or, food may be a way to cover up emotions that are too painful to face.

An eating disorder doesn't have to happen; at least, it doesn't have to progress beyond the early stages. As a parent, you are in a better position than anyone else to see what is going on in your children's life. You have the power, though you may not always realize it, to help them develop the independence and self-esteem they need to feel satisfied with themselves. You can actually help prevent an eating disorder from developing.

But your closeness to your children has its disadvantages, too. It is easy to get so caught up in your habitual way of seeing yourself and your family that even the trouble spots start feeling familiar and acceptable. Moreover, some of the social values that contribute to eating disorders are so common they seem normal, even admirable. But as a concerned parent you will want to consider how these destructive values are affecting you and your children. Ask questions and talk back—loud and clear.

The Seed of a Dangerous Idea

"My skinny little 12-year-old and her friends sit around pinching their thighs and reading diet books," complained one father at a recent parents' workshop. "Here she is, still carrying around her Cabbage Patch doll, and she's nibbling salads and passing up dessert."

Many youngsters start worrying about their weight as they approach adolescence. The reasons often go deeper than their wish to look like *Vogue* models. We'll go into some of these deeper reasons in chapter 3. For now, just remember that your children are taught to see slender 12-year-old bodies as normal. That new padding on your child's thighs feels like some kind of diseased growth to her. What the youngster needs to hear, first of all, is reassurance that she's not turning into a freak, she's turning into a teenager, and teenaged girls develop curves. It's an obvious fact, but a parent can easily forget that this is not obvious to a child reared on television commericals. She needs to know that she has a wonderful, healthy, normal body and that those skinny models are not healthy and normal—they are uncomfortable and half starved.

I also advise parents of a salad-nibbling daughter to sit down and talk with her in a matter-of-fact way about why she thinks she has to diet. Gently ask her, "What's this diet book all about, do you think? Where did you get the idea about counting calories? How do you feel about not eating any dessert?"

The seed of a dangerous idea—that she is not good enough—has been planted in her mind. The most helpful thing you can do is to let her talk about how she feels (no parental advice, please) and let her know with words and hugs that you love her as she is—not because she looks great in designer jeans, but because she's a unique person with wonderful qualities.

It is important to help your daughter celebrate her special qualities, not hide them. Television commercials and shows are telling her to dress, think, and act like everybody else, that it's awful not to be one of the crowd. Your job is to tell her, "You're special the way you are. You *are* good enough."

Focus on her special qualities. Does she have interesting ideas? Does she share her possessions with friends? Does she make people feel good? Does she love animals? By directing her attention away from her looks and toward her real self, you can help make her appreciate herself as a genuine person with a lot more going for her than thin thighs.

The last thing you should do is snatch away your child's magazine or diet book and give her a lecture on the dangers of malnutrition. But do let her know that your love for her includes concern for her health, and that a heap of raw veggies or a carton of yogurt is not enough of a meal for an active kid. There is no way you can watch every mouthful she eats—and the attempt could wreck your relationship with her in a hurry—but you cannot assume the diet kick will go away by itself. The idea is to find a middle ground and establish reasonable dietary expectations for your child to meet.

It's reasonable to expect your child to eat with the rest of the family; it's neither reasonable nor useful to make her clean her plate or eat things she doesn't want to eat. She needs to learn to make responsible food choices, but laying down the law at the dinner table won't help. You are doing your part by offering her good food, a friendly atmosphere, and a great big helping of love!

Prevention Starts with You

Another way you can help break the spell of the diet mentality is, first of all, to believe that your own body is okay. Don't expect your daughter to feel good about herself if you are forever counting calories and fretting over your weight. You are her model and her mirror.

The only way to be a positive role model for your daughter is to feel good about yourself. Prevention starts with you. Look at yourself and answer these questions honestly:

- Can you eat a piece of cake without feeling guilty?
- Can you wear shorts without worrying about how you look in them?
- Do you like yourself?

If you answered "no" to any of these questions, consider helping yourself first. A good way to start is by paying attention to the many putdowns you inflict on yourself daily: "Sure, I got the job but it was pure luck"; "All I do is procrastinate"; "I look like a mess"; "What a klutz I am!" If thoughts like these have become second nature to you, it is time to recognize that they reflect other people's judgments of you from long ago and that such thoughts are like slow poison.

Resolve to stop this self-destructive inner talk and start being gracious to yourself. When you accomplish a task, take credit for your skill and persistence. Draw up a "celebration list" of everything, big and small, that you have achieved in the past year and take time to congratulate yourself. When someone tells you how good you look, give them a big smile and a "thank you." When you look in the mirror, treat yourself like an appreciative friend instead of a critic.

A good self-help book (see *Suggested Reading* at the back of this book) can make you aware of the many ways you tear yourself down and offer further suggestions for building self-esteem. If you think you need the help of a professional counselor to start feeling good about yourself, find one. You and your child are worth it.

Let Your Body Be

"Start your blitz on fat now!" "Win the war against weight!" Such advertisements give the impression that it takes brute force to keep our bodies in any kind of shape at all. We are urged to mold them, firm them, shape them. We get nonstop advice on burning, melting, and fighting our fat.

But a growing number of medical researchers are saying we do not have to treat our body like the enemy to maintain a healthful weight and a good appearance. If we are in normal health, we don't even have to watch our weight, they say, any more than we have to watch our blood circulating. Given a reasonably balanced diet and adequate exercise, our body can be trusted to maintain—all by itself—the weight that is healthiest for each of us. This normal individual weight is called our *setpoint*.

Some of the best-known work on the subject of setpoints was presented by William Bennett, M.D., and Joel Gurin in their book *The Dieter's Dilemma* (listed in the *Suggested Reading* section of this book). They defined setpoint as the weight you usually maintain when you are not dieting or worrying about your weight.

You can probably remember a time in your adult life when your weight stayed pretty much the same, give or take a few pounds, over a period of several months or years without your giving it much thought. That weight is most likely your setpoint.

Medical professionals who subscribe to the setpoint theory—and most of them do to some extent—state that you can do three things about your setpoint: You can live with it; you can try to lower it by undertaking a regular, long-term exercise program; or you can try to outwit it by dieting. The first two choices make sense. The third is a foolproof recipe for frustration, and it can be dangerously addictive. Your son or daughter needs to know this. Knowledge is essential to preventing an eating disorder. By sharing your knowledge about food myths and the effects of diet and exercise, you can affect the way your family lives and how your children think.

One way to keep that wonderful, complex weight-regulation system on track is through regular exercise. You can help by planning to include some enjoyable physical activity as part of your family recreation. Some of us need more exercise than others to keep the self-regulation process working at its best, but even a walk to the neighborhood park or a game of table tennis after dinner would help—besides being a relaxing time to spend together. Kids who aren't wild about exercise may need some encouragement, but don't make a big issue of it. And be sure they have some say in the activity that is chosen.

Another way to help keep your family from dwelling on their weight is to promote balanced nutrition. You may first have to explode a few dietary myths. For example, many of the "starchy" foods—potatoes, bread, and pasta—that dieters shy away from are now endorsed by dietitians as essential to our weight-regulating process. A meal containing something "starchy" along with some protein and a small amount of fat and natural sugar keeps our stomach busy and contented for hours. One dietitian I know advises all clients with weight concerns to include an extra-good, chewy bread with their meals. (For some sources of up-to-date nutrition information, see the *Suggested Reading* section.)

You can also help by making meals as much fun as possible. Food that tastes good and is eaten in pleasant surroundings is satisfying. "Nutritious" food that kids don't especially like will just leave them prowling the kitchen an hour later looking for something tastier to eat. A relaxed eating pace is also important. Once you've prepared or ordered a meal that hits the spot, make sure everyone takes time to enjoy it.

"Now hold on a minute," you may be saying. "This is all well and good, but obesity is a major health problem in our country! Haven't studies shown that about 25 percent of our children are overweight? Isn't a low-calorie diet at 15 better than a heart attack at 50?"

News about overweight, out-of-shape youngsters hit the front pages recently, and is reason for concern. Most of the overweight children aren't getting enough exercise, and television is a leading culprit. A 1985 study showed that the prevalence of obesity in teenagers increased with the amount of television watched, by about 2 percent for each additional hour in front of the set.[1] Many kids are overeating because they feel bored and lonely. I believe these are the issues parents need to look into before deciding to cut back the calories.

If you think your child is seriously overweight, let her know that it's her health, not her appearance, you are concerned about, and get her to a pediatrician, family doctor, or registered dietitian. Typically, a medical doctor will take into account the child's general health and inherited body build before prescribing a weight-loss program. Even then, low-calorie diets are rarely pre-scribed for children and young teens. Personally, I would get a second opinion before putting a child on a drastic diet that leaves her feeling hungry. The effects of such a diet could be even more damaging than the excess pounds.

Encouraging your family to trust their bodies, get some exercise, and take time for good meals—are these guaranteed to maintain everybody's ideal weight? No reputable doctor or dietitian would make such a claim. But it's a method of weight control that is least likely to disrupt our body's natural functioning, not to mention the family peace.

Dieting and Other Unnatural Acts

Although 25 percent of our children are overweight, more serious grounds for concern is the number of normal-weight youngsters who are dieting to make themselves look like magazine models. Along with millions of adults, some will try anything, no matter how extreme, to achieve a body that fits their fantasies. Worst of all, they believe that their dieting is perfectly harmless because "everybody's doing it."

It isn't. It's very harmful. What's more, most of the millions who try dieting find it to be self-defeating. A low-calorie diet slows down the rate at which we burn calories so that our weight won't drop below its natural level. When that happens, we stop losing weight, get discouraged, and say the heck with the diet. As soon as we start eating normally again, our weight shoots up higher than it was before we started tinkering with the machinery. Some researchers think dieting actually raises our setpoint, creating that familiar dieter's lament, "I'm eating less but weighing more."

A raised setpoint is not the only problem. A too-skimpy diet keeps us forever hungry and dreaming of creamy concoctions. Binge eating is typically triggered by this self-starvation. Over-depriving ourselves seems to set off our body's safeguards against starvation, and it responds by wanting to eat as if there were no tomorrow.

But even though it is generally agreed that diets don't work, even though medical professionals have blasted them from Scarsdale to Hollywood, the pressures to diet are as strong as ever. Sometimes social pressures are even accompanied by threats of the loss of career or a vocation.

When 13-year-old Carrie started modeling school, her weight became an issue for the first time in her life. Not that she was fat—far from it. But young models-to-be are required to weigh in at the beginning of every class. Even if they haven't gained weight, they are constantly reminded that a few added pounds could spell the end of a budding career. The diet mentality is a "natural" part of a model's life, and Carrie learned it young.

As a figure-conscious new high school cheerleader, Beth found she could keep her weight down by vomiting when she strayed from her diet. She learned this from members of the wrestling team, who learned it from the coach.

Surprised? It isn't unusual for young athletes and dancers to be pressured to lose weight in drastic and dangerous ways. Most athletic coaches and teachers wouldn't go to such extremes as the one at Beth's school, but it's important for you to find out what your kids must do to qualify for sports and dance activities. If the weight requirements are strict, sit down and discuss with your child the pros and cons of participating. It's a hard choice for a kid to make—to be a successful athlete, dancer, or model, *or* be healthy. Do all you can to help your child choose health.

That's what Buddy did. Buddy, the young wrestler mentioned in chapter 1, eventually decided that the struggle of starving himself to make his weight before every match just wasn't worth it, and he quit the team. (An alternative would have been to enter a higher weight class.)

He didn't make that decision entirely on his own. Buddy and his teammates accepted the coach's demands without question. But his parents didn't. They made it clear to their son and to the school authorities that the weight-loss practices his coach was promoting were outrageous. Common sense, with a little help from Buddy's own healthy appetite, carried the day.

Ain't Necessarily So

Many kids think all books and articles on diet and health must be true because they're in print. You can do them a big favor by letting them know that writers and editors have no legal obligation to prove their statements are true. It's up to readers to separate fact from fantasy.

Most of us, of course, don't have advanced degrees in nutrition or medicine. How can we know what information is reliable? One useful resource is the current issue of a survey published every other year, by the American Council on Science and Health, which evaluates the accuracy of the diet and fitness articles in popular magazines. In its 1986 survey, the ACSH found that 76 percent of the publications they examined did a good job of presenting dependable information. But the articles in some of the most popular magazines—the ones teenagers especially enjoy, such as *Mademoiselle* and *Cosmopolitan*—were rated as "unreliable" or "inconsistent."[2]

Even without the help of medical authorities, you can help kids make sensible judgments about diet books and articles. You can teach them to be leery of promises that sound too good to be true. You can point out to them that many famous diet "experts" have no special training in nutrition and that the diets they promote have caused health problems ranging from fatigue to sudden death. Some are downright silly—"The Tex-Mex New Year's Diet" or "The Hot Gourmet Pizza Diet."

We all recognize nonsense when we see it. But deep inside all of us, young and old alike, is a belief in magic, to which all these books and articles appeal—that ever-blooming hope that changing our looks will solve our problems and make us happy. Break the news gently; you don't want to come on like the Grinch that stole Christmas. But don't let wishful thinking go unchallenged.

Let your kids know that the main goal of the magazines they pore over isn't to advise and inform and make them beautiful people—it's to sell advertising. Since most women's magazines advertise weight-loss products, their advertisers expect them to promote the diet mentality. Some do provide sensible, well-researched articles on nutrition and dieting, but the magazines should all be approached with caution.

In general, tell your young magazine reader to be wary of the following:

- Articles emphasizing the value of one "beauty food" or "wonder food" at the expense of a balanced diet.
- Diet plans based on "new scientific discoveries." They're usually untested findings presented as proven facts.
- Diets that promise quick weight loss (more than a pound a week) without hunger.

- Articles pushing vitamins and mineral supplements.
- Articles claiming that a particular combination of food is the key to weight loss.
- Diets that emphasize beauty as their goal without reference to health and nutrition.

A Look at the Great American Pastime: Snacking

When Americans aren't being sold on a new diet, we are being tempted to munch on something. It has been estimated that the average person is bombarded with about five thousand food commercials a year. Snacks can get to be a big issue in homes with teens. Certainly the overload of salt, grease, and sugar in those chili dogs, fries, candy bars, and milkless shakes is no bonanza to anyone's health. But kids *like* snack foods and they're a part of teen culture. Fighting over what your teenage children eat just takes away their responsibility for making reasonable choices and won't improve their diet a bit.

What is much more helpful, if your kid is stowing away great numbers of snacks, is to find out what purpose all this food serves in her life. What value does food have in your family? For most of us it has meanings that have nothing to do with nutrition. We often use food to help us handle our feelings.

Food as a Reward

"Just behave yourselves and you can each have a candy bar." "Get this room cleaned up or no dessert!" Most of us grew up hearing messages like these, and we send them to youngsters ourselves. Is it any wonder we make a connection in our minds between the kind of food we let ourselves eat and the kind of people we think we are?

Food as a Consolation

Babies cry because they are uncomfortable, aren't getting enough attention, or are angry or frustrated. Adults don't always know what's wrong, so the baby gets the bottle or the breast. Children who fall down and skin their knees get a cookie to "make it better." If our child flunks a test, fights with her best friend, or loses a class election, somebody is usually there with comfort in the form of something good to eat. Eventually, the connection becomes automatic: when we feel bad, we head for food.

Food as a Diversion

In a recent television commercial, a young mother is gratefully endorsing a certain brand of candy bar because, she says, it keeps the kids out of her hair (and her kitchen) until dinnertime. When children don't know what to do with themselves, parents may suggest that they play, watch television, or get something to eat. Eating becomes not only a substitute for a real activity, but a way to blot out the loneliness or boredom that drove them to the refrigerator for a snack. The real problem with using food as a diversion is that it becomes too easy to lose track of the feelings we want to forget. And to lose track of your emotions is to lose yourself.

I'm not suggesting that you try to stop your family from using food in traditional ways. After all, the connection between food and comfort is built into our culture. Besides, eating *can* be a relaxing form of fun. A delicious meal can make an otherwise awful day seem worthwhile. The idea is not to prevent kids from snacking, but to encourage them to do it as the result of a conscious decision rather than as a habit. When we munch from habit, it just makes us feel guilty and out of control.

How can you cut down on habitual munching in your family? Ellyn Satter, an authority on family nutrition, suggests some strategies. Keep cookies and other delectables off the counter tops—out of sight, out of mind. Don't snack in places where you normally relax or work, like bed, or your favorite easy chair, or your desk. Discourage lingering in the kitchen.

Instead of automatically chomping that candy bar or brownie, stop and consider how you feel. Encourage your kids to do the same. Help them see that food might make life seem better for a few minutes, but it won't make the bad feelings go away. It just keeps them quiet for a while.

Remind them that when they're tired, a short nap might feel better than food. If they're restless, exercise may be what they want. Sometimes you may just need to tell the children (and yourself) that a certain amount of stress in life is unavoidable, and eating can't change that. On the other hand, a piece of pecan pie may be exactly what's needed to feel a little better. In that case, Satter suggests, sit down and slowly, sensually enjoy that pie right down to the last gooey crumb.

Food as a Substitute for Feeling

Abnormal eating habits have nothing to do with a passion for pecan pie. Eating becomes a problem when it is used as a substitute for something else. Does your child habitually eat when she's bored and really needs stimulation? Does she eat when she's lonely and really wants to talk to someone? Does she eat when she's angry and thinks she has to "swallow" her feelings? Then she's using food in an unhealthy way. The snacks she gobbles on these occasions aren't the culprits; the food is nothing more than a release valve for tension and anxiety. Forbidding snacks won't help your kids learn what normal eating is. But what is "normal eating?" Ellyn Satter defines it as follows:

> Normal eating is being able to eat when you are hungry and continue eating until you are satisfied. It is being able to choose food you like and eat it and truly get enough of it—not just stop eating because you think you should. Normal eating is being able to use some moderate constraint on your food selection to get the right food, but *not* being so restrictive that you miss out on pleasurable foods. Normal eating is giving

yourself permission to eat sometimes because you are happy, sad, or bored, or just because it feels good. Normal eating is three meals a day, or it can be choosing to munch along. It is leaving some cookies on the plate because you know you can have some again tomorrow, or it is eating more now because they taste so wonderful. Normal eating is overeating at times: feeling stuffed and uncomfortable. It is also undereating at times and wishing you had more. Normal eating is trusting your body to make up for your mistakes in eating. . . .[3]

Avoiding the Pushy-Parent Trap

Your own healthy attitude toward eating will go a long way toward promoting a healthy attitude in your youngsters. But remember, eating disorders aren't only related to eating—they are a way to handle feelings. Anything you can do to help your child feel strong, competent, and lovable will help keep her from turning to abnormal eating habits.

I am convinced that most parents—certainly those of you who are taking time to read this book—try to help their kids feel good about themselves. It's easy to hurt a child's self-esteem unintentionally, though. How? By doing what you believe is your job as a parent—urging your children in the direction you want them to go—you can fall into the pushy-parent trap.

> One of my high school girlfriends got married last June. Just as I was walking out the door, my mom stopped me and said I was not going out in public looking like that—no makeup, flat-heeled shoes. She said I'd never be any kind of success unless I fixed myself up. And besides, I'd make the whole family look bad. I was so mad I could hardly talk. But I ended up putting on makeup and changing my shoes. *Carol, 18*

There's a lot of pressure in our society to set and attain high goals, and we want our children to do the same. It makes parents feel good to contribute to their achievements in every way possible, even if it means laying down the law occasionally. We want members of our family to be recognized as successful, accomplished people.

However, we may sometimes lose track of what we and our children really want, and become pushy parents. When that happens, family communications break down, and kids translate nearly everything their parents say into, "they don't really care about *me*!" Let's look at some of the messages that can cause this kind of misunderstanding.

We Only Want the Best for You

As members of a sports-minded family, my sister and I were raised on the virtues of competition: "Always do your best." "Never give up." "Anything worth doing is worth doing well." These were the family theme song. We always knew our parents really did want the best for us. They wanted us to develop our talents and learn skills that would help us succeed in life. But this kind of parental urging can be dangerous. Parents can get so caught up in their own ideas of what's best for their families that they lose sight of what their children may want.

Take Heidi, for example. At 16, Heidi is an accomplished cellist who plays in the school orchestra and a local chamber group. Her parents are classical-music buffs. Recently Heidi announced that she would like to take some guitar lessons. Her parents refused to buy her a guitar or to pay for lessons, though they were financially able to do so. Heidi's parents assumed that her goals were identical to theirs. While it is true that young people usually need strong encouragement to keep working on a skill as demanding as music, they also need your encouragement to talk about their own interests and goals. This lets them know you care about them as individuals. It tells them you respect their interests, even though these are different from yours.

Janine never felt that her parents listened to her, either. Wanting their first-born child to have the best of everything, Janine's parents steered her into gymnastics, ballet, and voice lessons—all the advantages they had never enjoyed. "I never learned to do anything really well," Janine's mother would tell her. "We want something better for you."

Nobody could accuse these parents of being uncaring. Still, Janine has spent most of her nineteen years feeling like a fraud, a failure, and an outsider in her own family. "We never talked about personal stuff," she says. "So I could never tell them the deepest sorrow of my life—that I wasn't the kind of successful, outgoing person they wanted me to be." Janine's parents, like Heidi's, were actually putting their own needs and wishes before their child's. They never sat down with their daughter and asked her what she wanted to do.

Your Life Is Our Life

Larry is angry with his parents most of the time. "I just wish they'd give me some space to live my own life," he complains. "If I go on a weekend church retreat, they want a play-by-play when I get back. And they're always on me about homework—even though I've been in honors classes since ninth grade."

Over-monitoring kids is an easy pattern to fall into; many adults grew up with the idea that being a parent means being in control at all times. Sharing power can seem especially risky to parents who place high value on what the neighbors will think. But sharing power can make life easier and more fun for everyone. You not only help your children take responsibility for their own mistakes, you encourage them to come to you for help when they need it. You are really saying "we want the best for you" in a way they can't misunderstand.

You'd Look so Nice, if Only . . .

I was really excited about going to Hawaii—it seemed like such a status thing to do. A few months before we went, my dad told me that if I could drop a few pounds, I'd have even more fun and wouldn't feel so self-conscious in my swimming suit. It felt like a bomb had gone off in my head—those words had such an impact on me. The only thing I thought about that whole summer was my weight. *Gail, 14*

My mom and dad never really said I should lose weight. I just knew that's what they wanted. When I started exercising two hours a day and lost 10 pounds, they acted like I'd won an Olympic medal or something. *Leslie, 18*

We may impose our own standards of beauty on our children simply by noticing and praising what is important to us. That is how well-meant praise can actually be destructive—a hard fact for many parents to accept.

Leslie's parents thought their praise would encourage Leslie to keep exercising and trying to look her best. Instead, it motivated her to keep losing weight until she had to be hospitalized. I can hardly overstress that praising kids for their looks can do as much damage to their self-esteem as criticizing their looks can.

Your children want your love and approval so much that they will go to almost any lengths to assure themselves of a steady supply. However, we don't have perfect control over how we look. We can't always be stylishly dressed or perfectly coiffed and groomed. Sooner or later, we all get old and wrinkled. When we are praised for something that's beyond our control, we feel guilty and phony. When your children receive praise for the way they look, they know your praise is superficial, and they're afraid it could turn to disapproval at any time.

No matter how much we value our appearance and our achievements, we all know there's a "real me" inside. What most of us are looking for, whether we're aware of it or not, is someone who can help us connect with that true self—someone who sees the unique human qualities that make us who we are. What your children need from you is recognition of their uniqueness.

I'm not suggesting that you ignore your children's tangible achievements or their pride in a new outfit to wear, but that you focus on the qualities that can't be taken away from them. All it takes is a brief sign that you noticed: "That took some courage for you to speak up for yourself like that, Susan." It's so easy, but we do it so seldom.

There are times when your daughter will come right out and ask: "How do I look in these shorts?" "Do you like my new haircut?" Young teens are extremely concerned about their face, figure, and clothes, and you certainly want to take their concern seriously. The idea, though, is to let them know you're proud of them no matter how they look. The exact words you say aren't so important: the feeling is. Your conversation might go:

"How do you like my hair this way, Mom?"

"I think it looks nice. Combing it back like that gives you a different look than when you curled it. I think it changes the shape of your face a little."

"Makes me look fat, doesn't it?"

"I think it brings out all your features more, especially your eyes. Makes you look a little older, too."

This isn't a judgment on how she looks. It's a straightforward response that shows you care enough about her to take an interest in her new hairstyle. If you're not crazy about what she's done with her hair, be honest:

"Do *you* like your hair that way? Then that's how you should wear it."

"You don't like it, do you, Mom?"

"No, but we have different tastes. Your taste is right for you."

If you really can't accept your child's physical appearance, consider talking over your feelings with a counselor. Your no-strings acceptance—and it can't be faked—is the most valuable gift you can offer your child. Her knowledge that you are proud of who she is will go further toward ensuring her success in life than any other advantage you can provide.

You Can Do Better than That

When Kara showed her A-minus/B-plus report card to her father, he tried not to be too enthusiastic. "After all," he thought,

"Kara is a very bright girl." He frowned and said, "Not bad. But you can do better than that."

Kara's father really is proud of her school performance, but he knows hard work and dedication are essential to success. He doesn't want his daughter to be one of those people who slide through life, never really working toward a goal.

But what Kara thinks is, nothing she does is ever good enough. The only time she gets rewards and attention from her parents is when she outdoes herself, which doesn't happen often. Perfection, after all, is impossible. And if perfection is the only acceptable standard, she's going to feel frustrated and incompetent most of the time. This does terrible damage to self-esteem.

Still, Kara does her best to act and look like the person she thinks her folks want her to be. In fact, she's become a fulltime people pleaser. In her endless search for unqualified approval, she is more intent on appearing happy and successful than being happy and successful. Somewhere along the line, she lost track of who she is and what she wants.

Put On a Happy Face

Parents who encourage their kids to be people pleasers and perfectionists aren't usually aware of what they're doing. Megan's parent's weren't. "When Megan was in second grade," her mother told me, "I sent an angry note to her teacher about the ridiculous amount of homework she was dumping on the child. As it turned out, Megan had *asked* her teacher for all that homework." She felt she had to do more work than everyone else in order to get the approval that she craved from her teachers.

Her mother also remembered that Megan always changed her clothes the minute they were slightly wrinkled. And she recalled that her daughter had told the family not to come watch her play basketball when she was in high school. "She was the fifth of five starters," her mother recalled, "but Megan thought that wasn't good enough. I don't understand it. We never said she had to be perfect."

But Megan's parents held her to impossible standards of another kind. Megan's mother came from a troubled family. Her parents fought constantly. She wanted a nicer home for her own children, so she insisted on "nice" behavior at all times. Arguing and shouting were taboo. She and her husband quarreled behind closed doors, and grumpy children were packed off to their rooms until they put on a happy face. Theirs was a peace-at-any-price family in which "bad" feelings simply weren't allowed.

What often happens in peace-at-any-price families is that youngsters don't learn how to identify their feelings. They may even learn not to have any feelings, just a sense of emptiness. Megan had filled the void in her life with rigid, perfectionist standards and an eating disorder.

The alternative to this family "peace" isn't open warfare, but it involves encouraging all the family, including yourself, to value the thoughts and feelings that come from inside—even when these feelings make you uncomfortable. Telling a youngster to put on a happy face or not to feel a certain way has the effect of telling her not to have feelings, and that is a powerful prescription for trouble. If you don't have feelings, you don't really exist.

Caution: Children Watching

> I remember my mother telling me how she used to cry almost every day in high school because she weighed about 200 pounds and had to wear old-lady dresses. I got a little chubby in seventh grade, and I was really scared. It seemed as though getting fat was the worst thing that could happen to a person.
> *Terra, 16*

Terra clearly saw that her mother hated herself as a fat teenager, and she assumed, logically enough, that her mother would hate *her* if she got fat. As a parent, you don't have to utter a single critical word to help instill the national fat phobia in your children. You make your attitudes clear in a thousand ways while your children are taking notes. Do they see healthy self-esteem or insecurity over weight and appearance? The following questions can help you decide. Answer with a "yes" or "no":

1. Do you discount compliments on your appearance, saying the complimenter was "just being nice"?
2. Do you think your life would be better if you were thinner?
3. Would you describe yourself as a frequent dieter?
4. Do you sometimes get into long conversations about diets and calories?
5. Do you feel guilty when you eat a rich dessert?
6. Have you ever compared yourself unfavorably to thinner friends or television models?
7. Do you avoid wearing shorts because you believe you are too fat?
8. Do you exercise mainly to "burn off" calories?

If you answered no to all these, congratulations! You're showing your youngsters what self-acceptance is. If you answered yes to more than two of these questions, consider seeking ways to improve your self-esteem that aren't related to your appearance.

Early Warnings

A young woman approached me after a talk I gave at a high school recently and said, "I don't know what to do about my parents—they're convinced I have an eating disorder. I don't! I lost seven or eight pounds since track practice started, but I eat three meals a day plus snacks. How can I get them off my back?"

The statistics on eating disorders are scary, and these parents were right to be concerned about their daughter's weight loss. But it's also important to keep in mind that the common warning signs can have a variety of causes. Just because your child shows one or more of the signs doesn't necessarily mean she will develop anorexia or bulimia. The main purpose of this list is not to alarm you, but to alert you to a void in your child's life. Does your child . . .

- Seem obsessed with her appearance?
- Do aerobic exercises for more than an hour a day?
- Make a habit of eating when she's sad or upset?
- Weigh herself once a day or more?
- Count calories or avoid snacks?
- Try to avoid eating with the family?
- Make abusive remarks about herself?
- Rarely talk back to you or show anger?
- Insist on being the best in everything she does?

By saying no to the diet industry's propaganda and the pushy-parent trap and by tuning in to your own and your youngster's feelings, you can do more than help prevent an eating disorder—you can help create the kind of atmosphere in which people grow. It may take some time and effort. It may mean letting go of some of your cherished beliefs about your role as a parent. It may even require some professional counseling. But wouldn't it be worth it?

Summary

This chapter has covered a lot of ground. It may be helpful to review the following key points:

1. Talk to your daughter about the healthy changes her body is undergoing as she enters puberty.
2. Trust and accept your own body. By setting a positive example, you will encourage others to do the same.
3. Understand that dieting is self-defeating.

4. Be alert to times when you or your child use food to drown out feelings.

5. Direct your praise at your child's unique inner qualities, not her appearance.

6. Let her make choices and mistakes.

7. Encourage your child to talk about her wants and needs. Talk about your own. Be honest with her.

Notes

1. William H. Dietz, Jr., and Steven Gortmaker, "Do We Fatten Our Children at the Television Set? Obesity and Television Viewing in Children and Adolescents," *Pediatrics* 75, no. 5 (May 1985): 807–12.

2. To obtain a copy, send a self-addressed and stamped (73 cents postage) envelope to the American Council on Science and Health, 1995 Broadway, New York, NY 10023.

3. Ellyn Satter, *How to Get Your Kid to Eat . . . But Not Too Much* (Palo Alto, CA: Bull Publishing, 1987). Reprinted with permission.

CHAPTER 3

I COULDN'T TELL ANYONE:

The Origins of an Eating Disorder

My teen years are kind of a blur—I was depressed a lot. I guess I gave the impression of being pleasant and kind, sort of a loner. It would have been a relief to be able to say, "Why am I feeling this way, Mom? I'm not happy, and I don't know why."

Jenna, 22

Most of the young women I see feel lonely and sad or angry, but it may take weeks or months of therapy for these feelings to surface. At first glance, many of my patients seem to have the world by the tail. They are charming, vivacious, accomplished, and popular. This is the mask they want to show the world.

We have a deep belief in our culture that people won't like us if we're not happy and smiling, and these young women have accepted that belief without question. As a rule, they are not purposely hiding their emotions, they simply aren't feeling them. Most of their energy has always been directed toward figuring out other people's feelings and expectations. These young women have always asked the outside world: "How should I feel? How should I act? What do I need?" They never learned how to seek these answers within themselves.

They know they're feeling pain, though—the pain of an aching void in their life. They feel empty, inadequate, unable to connect with those around them. Their isolation and emptiness make them especially susceptible to the pressures of growing up in our fast-paced society.

They are also at an especially vulnerable age. Most eating disorders occur just before or just after adolescence. Whether she is a preteen worrying about the new social and sexual demands of being a teenager or an 18-year-old about to leave home for college, she is in the midst of a time that is stressful for nearly every young person. The strain on a girl who doesn't know who she is or what she wants can be intolerable.

When a kid feels empty and unable to connect emotionally with family and friends, almost any major change, loss, or failure to meet her own rigid standards may find her unable to cope. Most commonly, these stresses are connected with school, peers, family, and her own sexuality. None of these pressures directly *causes* an eating disorder, but they put too much strain on a child who doesn't have the resources to face a crisis. As a parent, you can help by knowing which pressures may cause problems and how to recognize the first signs of trouble.

Honor-Role Blues

David comes from a family of high achievers. His older sister is a district attorney. His brother is a high-ranking Air Force officer. David figured the least he could do was bring home straight A's on his report cards. "I was a bookworm," he says, "into sports, band, all that nerdy stuff." He needed an appointment book to keep track of all his club meetings and practice times. What kept him going was a terrible fear of disappointing his teachers and parents. He felt he had two choices—either be the best in everything he did, or be a complete failure.

David became bulimic when he was a junior in high school. But even then he didn't realize he was under intolerable pressure during those years. He thought his joyless grind was just the way life was. He thought everybody lived in constant fear of failure. Food was the only way he knew of to relieve his tension.

Who was to blame? David's unhappiness was too complex to pin the blame on anyone. His parents certainly urged him to do his best, praised him for bringing home good grades, and failed to notice the signs of stress. His school must also take some share of responsibility. The child psychologist David Elkind thinks our schools are often guilty of pressuring some children beyond their ability to cope:

> Management programs, accountability, and test scores are what schools are about today, and children know it. They have to produce or else. This pressure may be good for many students, but it is bound to be bad for those who can't keep up. Their failure is more public and therefore more humiliating than ever before. Worse, students who fail to achieve are letting down their peers, their teacher, the principal, the superintendent, and the school board. This is a heavy burden for many children to bear.[1]

It's true that the need to achieve is a top priority in our culture right now. We've been taught to think of life as a racetrack and of people as winners or losers depending on how far and fast they can run. As the argument goes, we must put pressure on kids to achieve or they will fall behind and lose the race.

The drive to achieve is not necessarily bad for youngsters. There is a big difference, though, between the person who achieves because she loves what she's doing, and one who achieves because she's scared to death of failing. Even though kids are notoriously close-mouthed about what they're doing at school, they have ways of letting you know if they're driven by fear of failure. Consider your child's behavior and answer the following questions with a "yes" or "no":

1. Has she dropped activities she enjoys because she wasn't "the best"?

2. Is it hard for you to remember the last time you saw her acting silly, playful, or lazy?

3. Does she underrate her achievements in subjects or activities that come easy for her—as though they didn't count?

4. Does she become ashamed and upset if she gets less than an A on a test or assignment?

5. Does she look down on less dedicated classmates?

Even though she's not making unhappy noises, a child who does any of these things is not knocking herself out for the pleasure of it. You can help by not encouraging her to drive herself. Avoid pushy-parent behavior. Don't save your interest and approval for her high grades and trophies. Let her know you care about her ordinary everyday activities, things in which she doesn't necessarily excel. Encourage her to try something new just for the fun of it. Do whatever you can in your own life to prove we don't have to be "the best" in an activity to enjoy it.

I Don't Fit In

Social life is a major part of school. For some kids, it's *the* major part. School is where their friends are, and they're judged by their friends. To the child who doesn't have friends or doesn't feel like part of a group, lunchtime and the times before and after school are pure misery. This kind of isolation is especially rough on a young teenager because she desperately wants to fit in. What's more, her peers will have no mercy on her if she's different in any way.

Kelly can hardly remember a time when she wasn't being teased because she was fatter than the other girls in her class. Worse, the shops in the small Nebraska town where she grew up didn't carry girls' clothes in her size, so her mother sent her off to school in matronly doubleknits.

Even though the kids picked on her, Kelly felt lucky to get any attention at all. She was used and walked on. By the time she was in ninth grade, she was sleeping with boys from the high school because it made her feel more accepted. Then she started using laxatives to control her weight. Kelly doesn't remember where she learned to do it, and until now she never told anyone. It was her secret.

Hannah also feels like an outcast at school. Even at home she feels lost and invisible among her five brothers and sisters. Hannah has scoliosis. She has to wear a brace and undergo physical therapy once a week. She not only feels isolated because of her physical problem but guilty about the money her parents have to spend on her medical care. She doesn't date, has no close friends her age, and started bingeing and purging when she was ten.

Melinda's experience confirms a fear many children have about moving to a new neighborhood—that they won't measure up and fit in. Melinda is attractive and outgoing. She had lots of friends and activities until last year, when her father was promoted and her family moved to a more affluent neighborhood. The girls at the new school gave Melinda a cool reception and treated her like an outsider. The reason? She's "too fat" and her clothes have the wrong labels. The labels were easy enough to change, but Melinda is taking drastic measures to reduce her weight.

These young women never told a soul they were feeling unhappy until they sought help for an eating disorder. Young people may appear to be satisfied with school, teachers, and friends, may get good grades and take part in many activities, yet still feel deeply isolated. They may be working for those grades only because they think it's expected of them. They may not know who they are and feel afraid of failing. Often their friendships are superficial, and there's no one their own age with whom they can share their feelings. A common characteristic of girls who get eating disorders is that they don't know *how* to get support and enjoyment from friendships and social groups. And, though they're not necessarily quiet or withdrawn, they tend to let people walk all over them.

What can you do to help a child who may be feeling isolated?

The most important thing is to let her know that no topic of conversation is off-limits. Let her know there's nothing wrong with feeling discouraged, sad, or hostile. What I hear over and over from my patients is: "I couldn't tell my parents. They'd have been disappointed, or angry, or uninterested, or uncomfortable." Kids may assume you don't want to hear about their troubles unless you make it clear that you do.

It's also important not to make light of their troubles. A parent can minimize a kid's problems in several ways, most of them unintentional. One way is to cut short a tale of teenage sorrow with an instant solution ("Why don't you join the youth group at church?"), a wise saying ("To have a friend you must be a friend"), or consolation ("Next year will be better"). A common—and dangerous—way to talk a child out of a problem is to tell her, "Don't feel bad." A statement like this leaves her feeling more isolated than ever. It also makes her think she's abnormal for feeling as she does. Another way parents can minimize their child's problems is to zero in on the overeating issue when she turns to food for comfort. It's useless to address the food issue until you address the feelings that are driving her to stuff herself.

It's tempting to find instant solutions or talk kids out of their problems. It hurts to see a child unhappy, and natural to want to banish the problem as quickly as possible. But there are no quick and easy solutions for a child who is feeling lonely and unhappy. She needs to feel free to talk about her feelings, and she needs to know you are on her side, even though you can't solve her problem for her.

My Sister—Miss Perfect

Dora was always the one who was perfect in my parents' eyes. She's smart, cute, well-behaved, and comes home with straight A's. Once I got up the guts to tell Mom and Dad how I felt. I told them they treated Dora like a queen and me like dirt.

> They kept saying they love us both equally. But I can't stand
> the thought of being loved equally. I want to be loved more.
> *RuthAnn, 15*

Sibling rivalry is not always logical and not always out in the open, but it plays a big part in the lives of many of the young people I talk with. It's one of those experiences in kids' lives that can make them feel they don't measure up.

RuthAnn's jealousy of her younger sister began on the day her sister was born. She learned early that she could get her parents' attention away from little Dora by getting in trouble at school and by stealing money from her mother.

Meanwhile, little Dora saw her parents' disappointment in her older sister and tried extra hard to please them. The situation went steadily downhill, with RuthAnn acting out her bad-girl role and her parents blaming her for everything that went wrong in their household. (Dora continued to work hard at pleasing her parents. She's now anorexic.)

Toni also felt left out of the family limelight. She was bright and articulate, and her parents wanted to give her every opportunity to develop her talents. She was given lessons in dance and drama. But Toni didn't do as well in these activities as her parents hoped she would. She was also not much involved in school activities, and she didn't have many friends. "Finally," she says, "They just gave up on me."

Meantime, a little brother came along, and he began to fill the role her parents had groomed her for. He was good-looking, sociable, and athletic. He began to take up most of their parents' attention, while Toni depended more and more on food and television for consolation.

She recalls, "Bedtime was the worst. My brother and I went to bed about the same time. My dad would go in and say goodnight to my brother and talk to him for awhile. I'd lie there night after night and wait for him to come in and talk to me, but he never came."

Wendy feels she gets as much attention from her parents as her older sister does, but it's the wrong kind of attention. Wendy was always identified as the "cute" one in the family, the cheerleader. Her straight-A sister called her "dummy." Naturally, her sister was "the smart one" in the family.

Pasting labels on kids is another easy trap for families. It seems like good-natured fun, and may even seem like a way to reinforce children's strong points and help them achieve an identity. But to Toni and Wendy it was devastating. They become obsessed with their weight and their appearance. Toni says she feels like "a prepackaged person."

Despite the best of intentions, parents can't treat all their youngsters alike. It's not even desirable to treat them all the same because they are individuals. It's also a mistake for parents to think they are to blame for everything that goes wrong in their children's lives—sibling rivalry included. It's a good idea to remember, though, that your kids do compete for your attention and approval, and are constantly checking for signs of favoritism.

You can help a child who is feeling jealous and left out by noticing how much and what kind of attention you give each kid. Put yourself in the shoes of the others. They may never come out and tell you how they feel, but if there is intense teasing or quarreling among them, or if one kid is regularly acting up or withdrawing, you can bet there's trouble. Be aware that seemingly harmless comparisons between the children by friends and relatives ("You look so much younger than your little sister") can add fuel to the fire. So can teachers' comments ("Your brother Robert was one of our best students").

Why Did You Do This To Me?

My parents separated when I was 16, and I never told anybody how bad I felt about it. I pulled away from everyone, dropped out of school, and dieted until I was so thin my mother said I looked like death warmed over. But I didn't care. It sounds awful, but I just wanted to fade away and disappear. That way I'd be safe. *Cindy, 19*

Divorce has been blamed for all sorts of problems among youngsters, from low S.A.T. scores to drug abuse. It's true that some of my patients date the onset of their disorder to the breakup of their parents' marriage. But—I can't repeat it too often—none of these pressures in kids' lives actually causes an eating disorder. Those who are devastated by such crises are young people who, for a variety of complex reasons, don't have a solid sense of who they are. They're used to being what they think other people want them to be. They generally feel comfortable only when they're part of a group because they haven't learned how to function as individuals. If their group, particularly their family, changes, they feel lost.

Like Cindy, most of these troubled young people keep their feelings to themselves. They often blame themselves for what happened. Through magical thinking they believe they can cure the pain by changing the shape of their bodies.

Their feelings are never simple. They often feel angry and may want to punish the "offending" parent by making themselves ill. In some cases, they hope to put themselves in a position where they'll be taken care of like small children.

The loss of a family member or friend through death or just leaving home can bring about this same kind of deep, complex reaction. It's not uncommon for an eating disorder to develop when an older brother or sister goes off to college.

That is what happened to Paulette. She had never been especially close to her older brother Greg, but, as the family clown, he had distracted the family from a conflict between Paulette and her demanding father. With Greg gone, she felt more strongly than ever that she wasn't meeting her father's expectations. Mealtimes were especially tense, and she often went to the basement to watch television while her parents ate. For a long time Paulette's parents didn't realize she had stopped eating.

Stephanie is an only child who has watched her parents' marriage crumble over a period of several years. Her mother is obese and unhappy. Stephanie recalls one especially painful occasion when her mother reached over to touch her father's arm and he recoiled from her.

This 15-year-old girl feels responsible for her mother's happiness. She is torn between her wish to make up for her father's unkindness and her anger at feeling trapped in the situation. Stephanie's bingeing and purging act as a kind of smokescreen in her family, a focus of attention that keeps both her and her parents from having to look at their own anger, guilt, and unhappiness.

It's hard on everyone when things go wrong in the family, but it's especially hard on young teenagers. They are extremely self-conscious about how they and their family appear to the rest of the world. They're still young enough to expect their parents to be perfect, though intellectually they may know better. And they may have more trouble than a younger child in seeking reassurance and support because of their need to put on a show of independence.

The best way for you to help a child who has experienced a loss is, first of all, to notice what's going on in her life. Is she having problems with schoolwork? Is she sleeping or eating poorly? Uninterested in friends or activities she used to enjoy? Don't ask her what the matter is; she may not know how to put her feelings into words. Tell her you have a good idea of how she's feeling. That's a lot more reassuring than asking her to tell you, and it doesn't feel so much like an interrogation. It also gives her a good opening to let you know what specifically is bothering her.

When she's ready, let her express her feelings. She may be much more angry than you suspected. Be honest. If you have divorced and think you made some mistakes along the way, admit it. Let her know she is in no way to blame for what happened. If there's a problem in your marriage, seek professional help. Even painful experiences can help a youngster grow if they are treated openly. Children need to learn that problems can arise between people who are close, and that these are not necessarily anyone's fault.

I'm Not Ready To Be a Woman

Twelve-year-olds who diet may be responding to something deeper than the snares of Madison Avenue. They may be equating their new curves and body hair with a whole new set of challenges they are not sure they can handle.

In addition to the visible body changes, menstruation is a source of untold anxiety to many girls. "Sex and body functions were things you didn't talk about in my family," recalls one patient, "and I never felt comfortable being myself with the other kids. I felt like a freak when my period started at age 12. And there was just nobody to turn to."

Author Judy Blume, in her valuable book *Letters to Judy*, details the kinds of fears girls often have about the onset of menstruation— that they'll spot their clothing, that the boys at school will find out about their condition and make jokes about it, that they won't have the correct change to buy a pad from the machine in the school rest room and they'll be too embarrassed to ask the teacher for help.[2] Fears like these can haunt young teens, but they won't discuss them with you for fear of seeming stupid or—worse— weird. The books mothers often hand their daughters—the kind that explain only the reproductive cycle and menstrual hygiene— don't answer the many practical questions a young girl has about her coming of age. I'd recommend giving her, well in advance, a useful and delightful book entitled *Period* (See *Suggested Reading*). You can save her hours of solitary worry by anticipating her fears and helping her plan courses of action.

She may also experience deeper fears. Girls know that menstruation means growing up. It's the birth of their sexuality. It's reasonable for them to feel some anxiety over the approach of this change in their lives. For one thing, it means they won't be cared for as children any more. They'll be expected to be more independent. Fathers who treated them lovingly when they were small often pull back from showing physical affection as they show signs of maturing. I know of one father who made cutting remarks about teenagers and expressed regret that his little girl was turning into one.

Becoming a teenager also exposes young girls to all our contemporary pressures to date boys at an early age. They generally feel that they will now have to learn to please boys by acting flirtatious and looking sexy.

Certainly Kristin felt this kind of pressure during her early teens. Her mother had had face lifts and body reconstruction, and she told her daughter that maintaining a youthful appearance was necessary in order to attract and hold a man. Kristin developed bulimia at 14, when she started using laxatives, diet pills, and grueling physical exercise to control her weight. At 19, Kristin had a breast implant when her boyfriend criticized her for being flat-chested. When she recently turned 21, she underwent liposuction on her thighs, which she still considers too fat.

Not all teens feel ready to jump into the dating game. Some worry endlessly about not fitting in. Parents and educators should both be aware that sex-education talks and films, as valuable as they are, sometimes give young people the message that all teenagers date and that they are abnormal if they're not interested in, or interesting to, the opposite sex. This particular "should" can cause great unhappiness in kids who don't fit the mold. A young girl who deeply fears the demands of sexuality may even find her "answer" in anorexia, which halts the onset of adolescence and turns her clock back to childhood.

Why Didn't She Tell Us?

Looking back on the early stage of their child's eating disorder, parents sometimes ask: "What could we have done that we weren't doing? She was so hostile and withdrawn that she twisted every-thing we said into a criticism of her. Why didn't she *tell* us how she felt?"

Chapter 9 explores more about how to improve family commu-nication, but in the meantime it may be helpful to listen to what some of these young people say about *why* it was so hard for them to tell their parents what was troubling them.

What Would They Think?

A child may be unwilling to share deep feelings because of fear. If the family has spoken or unspoken rules against showing negative emotion, the children may not want to risk hurting their parents or losing their love by revealing pain or anger. They may also fear that their feelings are too different from other people's to be acceptable.

> I was raised to believe you don't show negative feelings. My teachers always praised me for being friendly and cooperative. My grandmother called me the Good Humor Girl because, she said, I was always smiling. I hated to let anybody see me cry. I couldn't imagine what my dad would have said if I ever got mad and talked back to him. *Cindy, 19*

> My mother is a wonderful, loving person. She had to go to work when she was 18 and never had much for herself. But she's worked hard to send me to modeling school and give me nice clothes. So I try to act cheerful even if I don't feel that way. It seems like the only way I can show her how grateful I am for all she's done for me. *Belle, 18*

> I've always felt different from other people, and I felt lonelier and lonelier as the years went by. I flunked a class in junior high and I was desperate to have somebody to talk to. But my feelings seemed so crazy to me, I was afraid people would think I was off the wall. *Rick, 21*

> I really get along well with my parents. They've always been nice to me, and they encourage me to do my best. But I worry a lot that they might get mad at me for something, especially my dad. He doesn't show his feelings much, so it's hard to know what he's really thinking. *Pauline, 15*

They Never Listen to Me

A complaint I often hear from young patients is that they are willing to tell their parents how they feel but can't get them to listen. In some cases, parents discourage their kids from speaking up because they feel the need to be in control at all times and are threatened by their child's assertiveness. In other cases, the family's hectic pace simply doesn't allow time for personal sharing.

> I was always getting lectures from my mom and dad, probably two or three a week. The three most-asked questions in our house were, how do we get through to you, what are we going to do with you, and is any of this sinking in? *RuthAnn, 15*

> My parents got scared about some of the things I started doing in junior high. They didn't like one of my friends because they thought she was too wild and crazy. So they wouldn't drive me to her house any more, and they tried to limit the time I talked to her on the phone. They thought they knew what they were doing, but they could have listened to *my* side once in awhile. It seemed as though all they were interested in was controlling me. *Lisa, 17*

> I get along okay with my parents, but my family runs a restaurant, and nobody ever has time to talk to anybody. It gets really crazy around here sometimes. Everybody says I'm very mature for my age, though, so nobody asks me how things are going. *Dave, 15*

I Never Knew You Could Talk About Feelings

The ability to share feelings with others is a skill that must be learned, usually from family or friends. Young people whose friendships are superficial and whose families discourage intimacy may not realize that talking about feelings can ease their anxiety and loneliness.

> This is the first time I ever talked about my feelings with anyone. I'm not even sure what you want me to say. Usually I just talk about people or school or things I do with my friends. *Kevin, 13*

When I graduated from high school, I flew to California to visit my cousin Barbara. She seemed to know something was wrong. She finally got me to talk about the problems with Mom's drinking and my weight. It was one of the hardest things I've ever done, but it made me feel better. I decided right then that the way to get your feelings across to people is to tell them! Before that, my way of telling people I felt bad was to shut myself up in my room and eat. *Candy, 20*

Behind the Wall

The media have tended to focus on the bizarre behavior that often accompanies anorexia and bulimia. As a result, those who suffer from eating disorders may seem to be making themselves suffer for no good reason. This makes them seem strange and different from the rest of us. They aren't.

An eating disorder is simply a way some people cope with their problems. Others may rely on alcohol or other drugs, buying new clothes, driving fast cars, or keeping constantly busy. Some of these ways of coping are more self-destructive than others, but they all serve the same purpose—to distract our attention from our real feelings so we don't have to face them and do something about them.

By the time a person has developed an eating disorder, her real feelings can be hard to get at because she's decided, consciously or unconsciously, that her feelings are bad or crazy and need to be kept hidden. How did she make that decision? Not necessarily because her parents treated her unkindly. Most of the parents I talk with are caring, concerned people. The process is more complicated than that.

Parents often forget that their almost-grown-up child doesn't think like an adult. She is experiencing new feelings she hasn't had a chance to test yet. When she's prompted to express one of these new feelings or to make some outrageous demand on you, she's not sure how you will react. If you show disapproval, discomfort, or anger, she's thrown off balance. If she gets enough negative responses, she learns to distrust her feelings and believe there is something wrong with her. She builds a wall to protect herself.

The wall keeps other people out. It keeps her from feeling dependent on others and gives her a sense of control. But living behind a wall makes her feel lonely and bored, no matter how sociable she may seem to be. That loneliness and boredom spell trouble. The eating disorder serves two purposes: it may ease her loneliness by gaining her the attention of others, and it gives her a day-in, day-out preoccupation that shields her from the bad feelings that led her to build that wall in the first place.

The feelings don't go away, though. Because they're locked away, they get magnified and distorted. Usually it is only when my patients are on the road to recovery that they can look back and talk about the feelings they couldn't tell anyone at the onset of their disorder. Let's listen to what some of them have to say:

> I guess I was a little lonely. The main problem was, I always felt so ugly! I thought my legs and waist were too fat and out of proportion. Then about a year ago I got sick and couldn't eat for three days. I noticed how nice and flat my stomach looked, and I thought, "I can look this good by not eating?" So I started making myself sick after meals. I tried using a Q-Tip, but I noticed blood after awhile and got scared. After that I just ate one meal a day, and it worked! It seemed like the first time I ever accomplished something. *Kim, 12*

> I started my period when I was 13, and I was very scared about what would happen to me. These things were never discussed in my family, and I was ashamed to mention it to my friends. I was very aware of my body and some of the kids called me Tubby. I guess that's why I started doing it. I tried to pretend it wasn't happening—skipping breakfast and lunch, having a little snack after school, and throwing up dinner. I was tortured by the fear that somebody would find out, because I knew what I was doing was morally and spiritually wrong. There was this one Bible verse I kept reading over and over: "Be sure your sin will find you out." *Bev, 21*

As soon as I started school I was in trouble. I never brought home a report card that didn't have a comment about my "poor behavior" or "lack of respect." I'd be a little afraid of what my parents would say, but at least they were paying attention to me for change instead of my spoiled-brat sister who never did anything wrong. Still, I never felt as though I should belong in that family because I'm a bad person and so different. I needed something to make me feel good about myself and accepted by my family. I picked my weight because I was starting to feel fat at that time. This is when I was 13. *Neil, 15*

I always felt as though people walked all over me, but I was afraid to speak up for fear of losing friends. I needed those people, even though they weren't very nice to me and made me feel like a fifth wheel. Even with my family I always felt like a visitor. When I was in sixth grade my dad said I'd have more friends if I lost a little weight. I decided to weigh 105 pounds, because I read about a model in *Seventeen* who was 5' 5", just like me, and that's what she weighed. I kept losing weight, but it was never enough. I still felt as though I was in everybody's way. *Kelly, 16*

I don't feel.
They can criticize me, laugh at me,
I don't get angry. I keep smiling.
I don't feel.

I don't feel.
It's because I'm empty inside.
If I could feel, I wouldn't need to fill the emptiness.
I wouldn't need to feed the endless hunger.
But I do.
They tell me to be good and keep smiling.
They tell me not to feel.
I don't feel.

Cindy, 19

These feelings make good sense to the sufferers behind their wall. Their feelings of guilt, anger, and rejection may not be an accurate reflection of what is going on around them, though. Yet in their isolation, it is natural for them to feel abandoned and helpless, regardless of what the actual facts of their lives may be. It's important for you to realize this, so that you don't let your child's feelings make you think you have failed as a parent. This is a common mistake parents make.

Another common mistake is to think the early signs of an eating disorder, including the moodiness and anger, are simply "growing pains"—something that will go away if you ignore it. It's true that a bulimic person's withdrawal may look like a teenager's normal need for privacy. But there is a difference of degree.

There is no harm in a teen's shutting herself in her room to dream or think or pore over her magazines. (They're her "how-to" manuals. They give her some of the answers she's desperately seeking right now.) You should be concerned, though, if you notice that she's pulling away from her friends and from activities she formerly enjoyed. These are signs that she has built a wall and is calling for help. You should also be concerned if you see any of the following early distress signals:

1. Have you noticed a loss or fluctuation in your child's weight?
2. Has she cut down on her eating?
3. Has she increased her level of physical activity?
4. Does she get upset when she can't exercise as planned?
5. Do you suspect that she may be vomiting after meals or using laxatives?
6. Have you noticed puffiness around her eyes? Bloodshot eyes?
7. Has she experienced a serious personal loss or setback recently?
8. Does she seem "not herself" lately—quarrelsome or touchy?
9. Does she seem overly concerned about taking care of others, especially fixing meals for others?

In chapter 4, we'll talk about what to do if you suspect that your daughter may have developed an eating disorder. For now, let me say that you can't drag her out from behind that wall by force. You can let her know you understand that she's hurting, though, and that you're there to talk about it when she's ready. The message you want to convey is that she's important and you care about her.

Notes

1. David Elkind, *The Hurried Child: Growing Up Too Fast Too Soon* (Reading, MA: Addison-Wesley, 1981), 55.

2. Judy Blume, *Letters to Judy* (New York: Pocket Books, 1986).

CHAPTER 4

BEHIND THE WALL:

The Advanced Stages of an Eating Disorder

It was Thanksgiving holiday and the refrigerator overflowed with food. My bingeing escalated. The food magically dulled the pain—kind of an emotional morphine. I felt as though I had set up a wall with my eating problem, which no one was able to overcome. At that moment in my life, I slammed the door shut on myself and everyone around me. My bingeing and isolation took on a new dimension with this decision. I used bingeing as a refuge from grief and guilt and unresolved conflicts with my father. I thought food and isolation would cushion me from the pain.

Jenna, 22

"She was always such a sweet kid—a straight-A student, considerate, so good with her little brother. Now she's like another person. She's hostile, sneaky, and impossible to live with." Most parents I talk with feel frustrated and bewildered over what's happening to their daughter. How did she get this way? How can she do such awful, painful things to herself? How can she do this to *us*?

There's more to an eating disorder than dieting gone berserk or a bad habit that's hard to kick. Still, the thought process isn't so different from what the rest of us experience when we get hooked on a bad habit. Take smoking, for instance.

If you've ever smoked, you may remember your first cigarette. It probably tasted like poison, made you cough, or even made you sick. But did you quit while you were ahead? Probably not. By the third or fourth cigarette you had convinced yourself that these nasty sensations were nice and that your smelly weed actually tasted good. Besides, it helped you relax and think better. Quitting—once the Surgeon General took all the joy out of smoking—felt terrible. You probably felt as though you had lost the very core of your personality. Maybe it even drove you to acts of desperation. An addicted colleague confessed that she once cleaned out her car ashtray at 3:00 A.M. in hopes of finding a smokable butt.

No habit-forming substance is involved in an eating disorder, as far as we know, but a similar kind of self-brainwashing takes place. An anorexic convinces herself that the pain of starvation feels good, and a bulimic looks forward to vomiting. "I feel horribly upset until I vomit," is a common remark. "Once the food is out of my system, I feel light and pure again."

Anyone who suffers from an eating disorder also feels ashamed and out of control. But she's able to blot out the evidence of her own feelings and think that it isn't really happening to her, or that everything will be all right tomorrow. As one young patient put it, "When you live with an eating disorder, you live with a lie."

If your child's eating disorder has progressed to this denial-and-doublethink stage, she will need help uncovering the place where she's hurting. This takes time, and it can't be forced. Meanwhile, it may help to look at some of the behavior typical of this stage, and the thinking that underlies it.

Just Me and My Shadow

By the time I was 13 years old, I knew I was headed for trouble. I didn't want to see anybody, even my best friend. I'd

> get all irritable and hyper when people were in the house with
> me. I'd think, "Please, would you just *leave?*" *Stephanie, 15*

A child with an eating disorder doesn't necessarily withdraw
into her room; she may become almost inseparable from her parents
(and some parents become inseparable from their child as the
disorder progresses). But she withdraws into herself. She creates a
little world that is ruled by strict laws of her own making. It's a
grim and narrow world, but it's one she becomes familiar with and
feels she can control.

I don't mean to suggest that persons with eating disorders are all
alike; far from it. But their thoughts and feelings are remarkably
alike in some ways. For example, nearly every patient I work with
feels an overpowering fear of losing control, along with the need to
be in control. Each one seems to be saying to herself, though she
can't usually put the thought into words: "*They* may rule my life.
But *they* can't take away the control I put on myself. I'm going to
be special, perfect, and I'm going to do it my way."

Once she makes this decision deep within herself, the next step
is to withdraw from all people and activities she can't control either
by self-discipline or by taking care of others. This may look like
delusions of grandeur, but it isn't. Her decision is based on a deep
self-distrust. Inside, she is not sure she can manage her own life.
And she feels that if she is not in complete control, she will lose all
control.

She's also very self-centered. She has the feeling that other people
are always watching her and disapproving of what they see. Such
thoughts as these make her fearful of being around others:

"If I go out today, people will stare at me because I'm too fat."

"I noticed some people laughing just now. I know they were
laughing at me. I've gained two pounds."

"When I see someone who is overweight, I'm afraid I'll be just
like her."

Anyone who has ever been alone for a long period may remember
how every little worry got magnified into a disaster. One reason for
discussing our thoughts and feelings with other people is to keep

them from getting blown out of proportion. If your daughter has an advanced, untreated eating disorder, she isn't sharing her deepest feelings with anyone. She has turned inward to the point where she's almost in a dream state. The beliefs she's developed help her to feel in control, but they don't make any sense at all in relation to the outside world.

It's Magic

Nearly all of us play magic games with ourselves sometimes, such as "if I make these next three stoplights I'll have good luck all day." Most of us perform little rituals every day, too. For example, you may follow a certain order when you get up in the morning— shower, dress, make coffee, get the paper—and feel a little out of sorts when the order is disrupted. When I was a kid I had a friend whose mother made a ritual out of cleaning her floors. If we happened to track a few drops of water into her gleaming kitchen, she'd be right there on the spot, paper towel in hand.

What all these private games and rituals have in common is that they have absolutely no consequences in the outside world. A few drops of water can't possibly ruin a kitchen floor. It makes no earthly difference whether I fix my morning coffee before or after I put on my socks. The only purpose of these personal routines is to help us feel in control of a small part of our world. They make us feel we're living up to a set of personal standards, and we get a vague feeling that we've let ourselves down when we don't follow them.

These are just mild examples of the kind of obsessive thoughts and compulsive rituals your anorexic or bulimic child may turn to in order to feel secure. The difference is that her rituals and routines occupy most of her time and she may feel like a complete failure if she doesn't observe them to the letter. She sees her routines as a kind of magic that can protect her from all the things she secretly fears.

To an anorexic or bulimic, eating is an intensely private activity, connected with shame and fear of losing control. Her routines protect her against that loss of control.

For example, an anorexic may start out by allowing herself only a certain number of calories each day. Then she may make a rule that the only foods she can eat are yogurt and fresh fruits. She may decide that each piece of fruit must be carefully divided into six pieces, or some other "magic" number, and arranged in a certain way on her plate. No food may be allowed to touch her lips when eating, or she may count to a certain number between bites.

Arrangement of personal belongings may also become a ritual. One young woman was in the habit of arranging her whole enormous wardrobe according to designer labels, and she became very upset if her order was disturbed. She also assigned herself a strict order in which her clothes were to be worn.

Physical exercise may be governed by strict rules and impossibly high standards. If she's determined to do one hundred sit-ups in fifteen minutes, her day is ruined if it takes sixteen minutes or if she's interrupted after doing only ninety-six sit-ups. What's more, she feels she has to keep beating her own record. It's not uncommon for a victim of an eating disorder to spend three or four hours a day in solitary running, sit-ups and push-ups.

Secrecy plays an important part in these rituals and routines. Your daughter won't be willing to discuss them with you until she's well along in the treatment process. Asking her why she is cutting and arranging her food peculiarly will only alienate her. For one thing, she's not fully aware of what she's doing. In the course of their treatment, my patients may be asked to watch a videotape of themselves eating. They are usually horrified at the strange habits they've formed.

A less obvious kind of magical thinking is the private theories many sufferers have about food, weight, and digestion. Bulimics may use laxatives on the false assumption that calories can be rushed out of the body and eliminated before being digested. (The fact is, food is absorbed mainly in the small intestine, which isn't affected by laxatives. In addition, laxatives eliminate water, not calories.)

Bulimics who vomit feel an unbearable tension after eating. Food feels like an impurity to them, something that can cause damage. They may go to extreme lengths to eliminate the food they have ingested. If they can't find the privacy to vomit right after a meal, they may even try to do so several hours later as a way of relieving their anxiety. Another common fear, especially among anorexics, is that eating will permanently stretch their stomachs. Only a board-flat stomach lets them feel that all is well.

Their thinking becomes more and more distorted as the eating disorder progresses and the physical effects of starvation or purging take their toll. The most common distortion is the tendency of most anorexics to see themselves as too fat. This delusion is partly the result of brain starvation. Hilde Bruch, a leading authority on anorexia, thinks sufferers may also brainwash themselves. They often spend hours in their room secretly admiring their thin bodies in the mirror to the point where their protruding bones start looking beautiful to them.[1]

I'll Show Them

When RuthAnn's mother first brought her in to see me, she said the junior high school counselor had reported that her daughter was stashing a bottle of Scotch in her locker and drinking it between classes. Apparently, she had been doing it for several months. How had she avoided getting caught for so long? "I kept a bottle of mouthwash in my locker, too," RuthAnn said.

It wasn't until RuthAnn actually showed up drunk for a gym class that she was confronted. But she wasn't especially upset when the principal called her parents. "I thought, great—this will really push their button," she later told me. Her father is a member of the school board.

RuthAnn, who has been bulimic since she entered eighth grade, blames her parents for her eating disorder and for her growing dependence on alcohol. "I wanted to be wild and crazy," she said. "All they ever wanted to do was control me, to keep me from making my own mistakes. I guess they thought they knew what they were doing."

RuthAnn's parents have been overcontrolling, a problem they're now working to overcome. They always wanted a complete run-down on her activities, and were always critical of her friends and dates. But it's also true that RuthAnn is using blame to deny the destructive things she is doing to herself ("I'm not doing this—*you* are").

Kelly also blames her parents for "making her bulimic." She always felt that her older brother got more than his share of attention in the family, and that she never got the love she deserved. By "sleeping around" and by getting herself expelled from high school, she hoped to get her parents' attention finally.

It is important to note that Kelly's parents care for her and are deeply troubled by her behavior. They had no idea Kelly felt unloved until she blurted this out in a family therapy session. This is often the case. The feelings that contribute to a child's eating disorder and antisocial behavior aren't necessarily caused by outright neglect or abuse. As often as not, they result from patterns of family behavior that the parents aren't even aware of themselves.

I Can't Help Myself

No one has yet shown that food is an addictive substance. But it's no easier for a bulimic to control her urge to binge than it is for an alcoholic to pass up the bottle. It's also true that many bulimics, like RuthAnn, also get involved in alcohol or drug abuse.

Many bulimics also become shoplifters. Lynn, for example, started shoplifting supermarket food with her friends when she was a junior in high school. She got hooked on the excitement of getting away with it and soon became more daring.

Our big thing was to go out and shoplift anything we could get our hands on. We would get food, jewelry, records and tapes, stationery, books, or makeup. One of the guys would go into a store, rip off a $30 bottle of White Shoulders perfume and return it the next day and get the money back. Half the stuff we didn't even need. We just liked the thrill.

Shoplifting is another way bulimics express their low opinion of themselves. They feel they need something, but they don't think enough of themselves to believe they deserve it. So they steal. Eventually they get caught, though, and the shame they feel is usually strong enough to make them seek help.

Mind over Matter

People who suffer from eating disorders experience terrible emotional and physical pain, but they also experience rewards. As one patient wrote in her journal:

I usually binged late at night so as not to interfere too much with my social life. But I also remember that my in-vogue thinness and my newfound control over my parents made me more confident of myself, and I began to receive respect from the others at school.

The payoff for all their suffering is the feeling of being powerful and special. This may be the first time in their lives they have experienced these good feelings, and so their physical discomfort seems a small price to pay.

All winter I slept with the window open and just my underwear on. I heard the body will burn more calories if it's trying to keep warm.

Last year I was taking twenty-five Ex-Lax a day. The pain got pretty bad sometimes, but it was the easiest way I knew of to control my weight.

I was cold most of the time. Even when it was 80 degrees out,
I'd curl up and watch television with a blanket and a hair dryer
to keep me warm.

These young women achieved their victory of mind over matter by denying their own feelings. They simply pretended that certain things were not happening to them, or that everything would be okay tomorrow.

How Long Has This Been Going On?

Parents are often unaware of their child's eating disorder until it has reached an advanced stage. This is partly attributable to our human tendency not to see things we don't want to see. But this also happens because those who suffer from eating disorders are masters of deception. They do everything in their power to keep their behavior a secret.

They may make excuses for not eating with the family, saying that they have already eaten, or are not hungry, or have been invited to eat at a friend's house. If they are bingeing and purging, they will plan to do so when they are home alone or will find ways to disguise their actions.

Another reason parents may not recognize their child's eating disorder is that it doesn't always fit the symptoms described in the magazine articles. Instead of starving themselves or bingeing and purging, some sufferers abuse their bodies with rigid diets and excessive exercise.

Take Tracy, for example. When she was 14 she started taking diet pills to help her get rid of her "peanut-butter fat." The pills kept her fidgety and sleepless, so she started experimenting with diuretics and laxatives. She also fasted, sometimes for two or three days at a time, and exercised in her room for two hours every evening.

The cravings produced by the fasts drove her to periodic eating binges that lasted several days. These were followed by ruthless dieting that made her lose the 10 or 15 pounds she had gained. She thought about food during all her waking hours.

Tracy's parents didn't detect her disorder until she was a high school senior. She was doing well in school and she managed to hide her chaotic eating behavior and her weight fluctuations from her family. They were a family that didn't usually eat together or, if they did, they watched the news or read the paper. It wasn't until the family food bills got out of hand that they realized something was seriously wrong.

The first reaction of many parents, on learning that their child has an eating disorder, is to ask: "What did we do wrong? How did we fail?" My response to these parents is: You've done your best. The causes of your child's disorder are complex. It's likely that some aspect of your family life is creating a problem for her which she can't, for some reason, communicate to you directly. In any case, you can help your child more by thinking of this undesirable feature of your family life as a problem with communication and attention, rather than as a personal sin.

The guilty feeling "what did I do to my child?" often keeps parents from responding to her disorder as wisely as they might. Later on, we'll talk about helpful things to do and say. First, let's look at some nonconstructive responses.

She Must Be Going Through a Phase

Parents sometimes react to their daughter's destructive behavior by pretending it isn't happening. Denial of family problems is one of the most frequent responses I see in family therapy. It's not hard to understand why. You love your child, you want her to be happy, and so it's painful to let yourself see that she's in trouble. You may feel that her unhappiness reflects on you and on the quality of your family life. You may fear that confronting her will only make her worse. But denying the problem is always harder on a child than confronting her.

"The first time I made myself sick after dinner, my dad caught me," reports one young patient. "I thought, here's a way to get their attention, anyhow. But after awhile they just ignored the whole thing. I guess they hoped it would go away. I felt incredibly isolated."

At age 10, Joya started stealing money from her mother's purse to buy snacks on the way home from school. When a neighbor got suspicious and told Joya's mother, she politely told the neighbor to keep her nose out of the family's business. No one mentioned the matter to Joya. It seemed like something she'd grow out of. "And she was always so angry," her mother later told me, "I never knew what to say to her."

Marti had graduated from high school and moved into her own apartment, but she still stopped by home two or three times a week. She usually came by when nobody was at home. In fact, no one would ever have known she was there, except that her younger sister would announce to the family, "Marti's been home again. The fridge is empty." Her mother's reaction was, "I'm glad Marti always feels welcome here." She never said a word to Marti about the missing food.

A parent's failure to see, understand, and confront makes the child with the eating disorder feel even more alone than she does already. It also allows the problem to become increasingly serious.

You're Not Doing That Disgusting Thing, Are You?

Donna felt that she'd never succeed in keeping up with her two sisters. One sister just opened up a dance studio, and the other was whizzing though law school. Donna's biggest fear was looking like a failure to her mother.

She kept her bulimia a secret throughout her first two years of high school. Finally, her guilt became so intense that she resolved to break the news to her mother. She arranged to meet her mother at a restaurant to avoid an unbearably emotional scene.

Donna wrote and rehearsed her "speech" well in advance. It kept her awake every night for a week. When the moment arrived, her nervousness made her talk so loudly that everyone in the restaurant must have heard what she was saying. When she finished, her mother had tears in her eyes. "I can't believe you could do that disgusting thing," she said, failing to notice Donna's courage and pain.

For many people, eating disorders are still a taboo subject, partly because they are not widely understood. Public education programs have made it clear that kids addicted to drugs and alcohol are suffering and need treatment. An eating disorder, on the other hand, is perceived by some as a nasty form of self-abuse by spoiled kids who have everything going for them. It's not only heartbreaking for a parent, it can be embarrassing.

But a parent's disgust is destructive to a child's self-image. It only reinforces her own feeling that she's a bad person who does horrible things. Her problem won't begin to get better until she can say: "This is something I do. I don't like it, but I'm beginning to like me, anyhow." And she can't say that until you can look at her behavior without flinching.

Just Use a Little Willpower!

It was Joanne's stepmother, Sylvia, who first discovered something was wrong. She walked into her stepdaughter's room one day as Joanne was trying on her new swimming suit, and she was shocked at the sight of those protruding bones. She also noticed for the first time how dull and brittle Joanne's hair had become.

Sylvia had always made a point of talking things over with her stepdaughter, and she told her how worried she was. She made an appointment with the pediatrician for the following week.

Joanne's father was less supportive. In fact, he was angry. He was the kind of man who prided himself on strong self-discipline, and he expected the same from his family.

"She needs to eat, that's all," he told his wife. "She doesn't need a doctor for that, does she? If you didn't cater to her so much, this wouldn't have happened."

Blame and anger are common reactions to the feeling of helplessness. But blame never solves problems, it only intensifies them. One of the reasons many kids hide their disorder is fear of a parent's anger. Like denial and disgust, blame slams a door in your child's face and leaves her stranded—a sure way to damage your relationship with her. It is better to think of an eating disorder as a "no-fault" problem.

You Just Need to Gain a Little Weight

When Pattie became anorexic at age 15, her mother told her to start eating and gain some weight, or she'd have to go into the hospital and be fed intravenously. That scared Patti into eating and gaining back the 20 pounds she had lost, but it didn't change her feelings about herself. She couldn't give up dieting or her need for rigid control.

It didn't help matters when her mother said, "'You're okay now. You don't have to gain or lose any more weight." Patti resented her mother for saying that—it seemed as though her mother worried only about Patti's weight and looks. She didn't seem to care about how Patti felt. "I knew I wasn't okay," she said. "I didn't like myself. I still felt isolated and rejected by my family."

Because severe weight loss is a threat to a child's health, food and weight are usually the issues parents focus on when they learn of their child's eating disorder. But it's important to remember that eating disorders are not primarily about food. They nearly always reflect other problems—difficulty in expressing feelings, poor self-esteem, or trouble in dealing with a loss or change. Focusing on her food abuse and weight loss means you will miss out on the deeper issues that are making her feel awful. You'll also make her feel that no one on earth can help or understand her.

How Can I Help You?

Rae's parents had always been there when one of the kids was in trouble, and they intended to do all they could to help Rae through her bulimia. They hadn't noticed the changes in her appearance and behavior until she fainted in school one day. But at that point they wasted no time in confronting their daughter and letting her know they were on her side. "Tell us how we can help," they pleaded.

Terrified as Rae was of having her behavior discovered, it was a relief, too. It made her feel a little less alone. But she was in no position to tell her parents how they could help her. She didn't even know what she needed at this point.

"Tell us how we can help," seems like a caring thing to say to someone who is in pain. The fact is, it's frustrating to a child with an eating disorder. It's a way of telling her you feel helpless, and she'll pick up on that. She's already feeling helpless herself, and the last thing in the world she needs is helpless parents. Better to learn as much as you can about eating disorders and be as confident as possible.

How Can You Help?

The best way to avoid the pitfalls in confronting a child with an eating disorder is to understand her underlying feelings of incompetence, guilt, and fear. Asking her to give up her destructive eating behavior and gain weight is asking her to give up the one thing that allows her to feel in control of her life.

That doesn't mean you should stand by and do nothing. Tell her directly that you're concerned about her and want to help. Parents often think kids take their love and concern for granted, "because of all the things we do for them," but that isn't necessarily true. Tell her you want to help (but don't ask her how). Tell her you've noticed that she seems unhappy, and ask her if she wants to talk about it.

At first she may not want to, and you should respect her wishes. Remember her fears. If you try to force her to talk to you before she is ready, she will interpret your concern as an attempt to gain power over her and may shut you out completely.

Contradicting her and pressuring her with a lot of questions can have the same effect. If a kid says, "I look fat," it won't help to say, "No you don't." It won't help to ask, "Why do you feel that way?" She doesn't know, and she'll feel as though you're interrogating her. Better just to state your feelings: "I'm sorry you feel that way, but I don't think you're too fat. If you want to talk about it, it's okay."

When she's ready to talk, listen. Do not offer judgments, criticism, or arguments. Encourage her to share her thoughts and feelings, particularly on topics not related to food. Above all, don't give advice. "I hate it when my parents give advice," is a common complaint. "I feel as though they're not really seeing me—just my eating disorder."

Praise can be tricky for the same reason. It often sounds calculated, especially comments like "you look so much better since you gained some weight." Your daughter will either think you're trying to manipulate her or she'll think she's getting too fat and start dieting again. Better to say something unrelated to her weight and appearance, along the lines of "I like talking with you—you're fun to be around."

If you're confronting her for the first time, you might say something like: "Karen, I've noticed some changes in you lately—particularly in your eating. You seem to be a little down, too. I care about you a lot, and I'm concerned. Sometimes when we're sad or upset we take out our feelings on food. This is what's concerning me now. I know there's a lot of pressure to be thin, and some people control their eating too much, or they throw up. Is this happening to you?"

If she says "no" and says you're crazy for asking, she may not have the problem you suspect. On the other hand, she may have the problem and be afraid you will think she is crazy. Don't pressure her. Say "Okay, I'm just kind of worried about you. If you ever want to talk about anything, we'll work together on it."

If she says "yes," you've made an important breakthrough in communicating with your daughter. She has begun to trust you and to ask for help.

Another strategy recommended by many professionals for confronting your child for the first time is to give her some factual information on eating disorders that she can read in private. (See the *Suggested Reading* section of the book.) You can then talk with her when she's ready.

Advanced Distress Signals

As I mentioned earlier, no one ever discovered that she developed anorexia or bulimia overnight. The distress signals are there all along, though they get more insistent as time goes on. It *is* painful to admit that your daughter is in trouble, but ignoring the problem never works. If your child shows any of the following symptoms, get professional help for her—now.

1. Has her weight dropped or fluctuated noticeably? Remember that weight loss takes a long time to show up in the face.
2. Have you noticed any of these changes in her physical appearance: dry skin and hair? puffiness and blotches around her eyes? swelling at the angle of her jaw?
3. Has her menstrual period stopped or become irregular? Have you noticed evidence of bloating that is not caused by premenstrual tension or some other medical condition?
4. Does she get panicky if she can't exercise as usual?
5. Does she need extra blankets and clothing even in mild weather?
6. Is she regularly making prompt trips to the bathroom after eating?
7. Is she hiding food? Performing little rituals with her food at the table?
8. Have you found unusually large numbers of food

wrappers or containers in the trash? Is food often missing
from the refrigerator or pantry?
9. Has she been unusually depressed or irritable over an
extended period of time?

Remember that she thinks her painful symptoms are a small
price to pay for her feeling of "specialness." She may not complain
about feeling unwell—in fact, she may act unusually energetic and
continue to do well in school. Don't be misled—these distress
signals are silent appeals from behind her wall. She wants you to
face up to her eating disorder and take care of her.

Notes

1. Hilde Bruch, *The Golden Cage: The Enigma of Anorexia Nervosa* (Cambridge, MA: Harvard University Press, 1978; Vintage Books, 1979), 144.

CHAPTER 5

WALKING ON EGGS:
Coping With an Eating Disorder in the Family

We know now that Pam is throwing up to get attention, but it's hard for us to understand why she has to do this. We have our family problems just like everyone else, but we all care for one another, and we used to have fun together. Now we're at each other's throats most of the time, and it's getting worse. We need help!

Steven, Pam's father

Recovering from an eating disorder can take months, even years. This period can take a heavy toll on your family. Food, fat, and your child's mood swings can come to rule your lives. You worry constantly over your daughter's health. You may feel isolated from normal life, and wonder at times if the fun has gone out of your life for good.

The hardest part may be comparing the way things are now to the way they used to be. Pam's family, for example, was always active and fun-loving. The whole family—mother, father, Pam, and two brothers—runs a prosperous horse-breeding business. They work together, love their work, and love each other. Until Pam became bulimic, they had no reason to suspect anything was wrong.

But once they discovered their daughter was in trouble, they did something that is typical of healthy families—they faced the problem head on. They said, "Pam is one of us and she's hurting. We'll do whatever it takes to find out what's gone wrong and help get it corrected."

This sounds like the obvious way to cope with family trouble, but it's not easy for everyone to respond the way Pam's family did. It can be painful to look at the way you've always interacted as a family, let alone face up to making changes. Many of us enter adulthood and parenthood with negative feelings about ourselves that make us distrust our instincts. We hide behind a mask of how we think we *ought* to be. Then, when trouble strikes, our first thought is not "What's the best solution?" but "How can I keep things the way they are? How can I protect myself from all this pain?"

Families like Pam's face the facts honestly, talk about them, and pool their resources to support the member who is in trouble. Families who adopt unhealthy ways of coping try to sidestep the problem, in hopes that it will disappear. Their good sense and compassion take a back seat, and they blame one another or get paralyzed by guilt. These reactions are human and understandable, but also very painful to live with. In this chapter, we will explore some unhealthy coping mechanisms so that you can recognize them if they are happening in your family.

Let Me Save You!

My eating disorder makes my mother angry and upset at times. She thinks it's her fault, and she keeps asking the therapist, "What can I do? What can I do?" But she's doing everything she can. I just wish we could be friends and she could feel safe and blameless. It's really not her fault I'm this way. *Allison, 17*

Allison's mother feels the way parents of a young car-accident victim often feel: We shouldn't have let her drive so young. We should have warned her more about the dangers. We should have driven her ourselves. And so on. These feelings go on nonstop and take a terrific toll on personal happiness and relationships with others. Guilt and self-blame are like a full-time job with plenty of overtime.

As a parent, it's hard to avoid guilt feelings altogether; they are closely associated with your wish to help your kids and to avoid hurting them in any way. The trouble with guilt is that it isn't focused on the person who needs the help, though it may feel that way. It's really focused on you and your feelings. Allison's mother keeps saying, "What can I do?" but her energy is so tied up in feeling guilty that she can't help her daughter. What she's trying to do is single-handedly save her.

What's wrong with trying to save your children? As a parent, aren't you responsible for your children's happiness? Shouldn't you do all you can to solve their problems? No.

Trying to solve a child's problem, particularly when the child has an eating disorder, does more harm than good. It takes away the person's sense of control—remember, it's the feeling of having no control over their lives that torments most sufferers of eating disorders. The sense of powerlessness undermines the person's feelings of self-worth and competence. Most important, though your child may act helpless or crazy at times, she is neither. She needs to learn that she can ask for support, but can't depend on others to fix her life. Your job as a parent is to give the support needed to help your child solve her eating disorder, not to try to solve it for her.

It may not be easy to tell the difference between giving support and trying to save someone. It seems to be part of the American character to think there is a solution for every problem and that we have a sacred duty to figure it out. It's very hard for most people merely to be with someone who is having trouble. It makes people feel inadequate as parents and as human beings to sit down by someone who is hurting, put an arm around her, and simply listen. We all want to *do* something.

This desire to do something can lead parents to get over-involved in their child's life. Some parents of children with anorexia or bulimia put their own lives on hold and try to act as nurse, pal, and police officer around the clock. They try to watch every bit their child eats or doesn't eat. They know who she's talking to on the telephone; if she goes out, they expect a full report when she returns.

They feel that they know their child through and through—or did, before she developed her disorder. Sometimes they even try to express her thoughts for her. Allison's mother does all these things. She's a caring woman, and she wants her daughter to be healthy and happy. What she doesn't see at this point is that trying to save Allison is really a way to help herself feel less guilty and inadequate. She's not looking clearly at what her daughter needs.

Count Me Out

How about Allison's father? What is he doing while his wife is trying to save their daughter? He's feeling angry—with Allison for "wrecking" the family and with his wife for catering to their daughter's "craziness."

Allison's father was raised to believe any problem can be solved by hard work and determination. He often asks Allison, "Why don't you stop what you're doing? You look fine. What's the problem? All it takes is some willpower."

It's not that he doesn't care about his daughter—he does, deeply. But, like his wife, he's feeling bad. He never learned to show his feelings because that wasn't allowed in his own family when he was growing up. Hard work and providing the family with nice things were what counted. Now, as he watches the family he's worked hard to provide for crumbling around him, he sees only an ungrateful brat with idiotic notions about staying slim and a wife who is insisting that the whole family get their heads examined.

Allison's father did come to see me, once. As we got into the subject of his feelings toward Allison, he came close to tears. He let his mask slip for an instant and it hurt too much. I never saw him again.

Allison's father supports her therapy, grudgingly, because he knows her health is in danger. But his anger and lack of involvement take a toll on him and the rest of the family. He's avoiding the pain of changing, but at the high cost of alienating his daughter and his wife. Allison will get better because she's gradually learning to distance herself from her father and take care of her own needs. It's not a happy outcome, but it's the healthiest one for Allison at this point.

In a number of the families I see, one member seems to be saying, "count me out." There are other ways of conveying this message besides casting blame or refusing to take part in the treatment. One girl's parents regularly came to the therapy group but tried to keep everyone entertained with their witty banter. Finally, their daughter told them not to come if they didn't want to be involved—they got the message and changed their approach. A parent can also avoid the problem by getting immersed in work and being away from home a lot. Looking for instant solutions is another way of shunning the problem and avoiding the pain of change. Instant solutions usually begin with the words "You'd be fine if only . . ." They never solve a thing.

Let's Pretend She Isn't Here

Parents aren't the only family members to say "count me out." Brothers and sisters can't help being affected when one family member starts causing problems, and anger is a common reaction. Anger can be healthy and useful, but too often it takes the form expressed by Shelley's two younger brothers.

Shelley's brothers were genuinely worried about their anorexic sister, but they were also embarrassed and not used to expressing their feelings. They were afraid they may have been partly to blame for their sister's disorder. Maybe they'd said or done something to hurt her? They couldn't bring themselves simply to say, "We're worried about you." Instead, they channeled all their feelings into anger and avoided Shelley as much as possible. When their feelings got too strong for them to handle, they complained to their mother about their "crazy" sister and how disgusted and ashamed they felt. Their behavior went beyond "count me out"; it was more like "Let's pretend she's not here."

It's not unusual for brothers and sisters to feel ashamed of being seen in public with an anorexic family member. As teenagers, they are painfully hyperconscious of public opinion and what they imagine it's saying about their skinny sibling. They feel humiliated by the stares of strangers and their insensitive questions, such as "is your sister going to die?"

The anger and confusion of these family members is understandable but hard on everyone. It hurts the person who's suffering from the eating disorder and who needs all the support she can get. It also hurts those who pull away from a family member who needs help. Moreover, withdrawing from those who need support can get to be a habit that will cause serious problems in relationships later on. How can anyone have deep and lasting relationships if they've learned to say "count me out" or "let's pretend she's not here" when differences and difficulties arise?

An even more destructive way for a youngster to back off from the eating disorder of a sibling is to say "let's pretend *I'm* not here." This is the position taken by Ellie's 10-year-old brother, Doug. Always quiet and well-behaved, he never shows any anger toward Ellie's bulimia and bad moods, as his two older sisters do. Doug goes to his room when a family fight is brewing and other times as well. He builds model airplanes, reads, or does his homework. He often goes to a friend's house to watch movies on their VCR or have dinner. The kid who plays the game of "let's pretend I'm not here" usually succeeds in being ignored. He never causes any trouble and never tells anyone how angry and hurt he feels. However, he needs help, too.

Looks Like a Good Idea to Me

Though family members usually view the anorexic or bulimic with a mixture of anger, pity, and alarm, younger siblings sometimes look up to her. They may even try to imitate her. Like Nancy's little brother, for example. When Nancy's parents insisted she come to the table and eat with the family, Nancy played with her food and ate almost nothing. Her excuse, finally, for not coming to the table at all was that her 2-year-old brother started refusing to eat, too. This scared both Nancy and her parents so much they finally agreed to let her stay in her room at mealtimes.

At much greater risk are younger sisters who see their older sibling's eating disorder as a neat way to stay thin. There's no denying that some young people think an eating disorder is glamorous. It sets a person apart. It suggests daring and self-discipline beyond the reach of ordinary people. In a society that glorifies ambition and self-denial in achieving goals, these perceived qualities carry a lot of power.

While I don't agree with the recent *Newsweek* statement that eating disorders are "a cult that's sweeping the country," it is true that young people do sometimes pick up that idea from others. In college dorms and in group homes for troubled teenagers, some young women swap techniques and develop "barf buddies." Most experiment with fasting or purging purely as a weight-loss gimmick and won't persist. But there is a danger that this behavior will persist when slimness and "specialness" are prized by family and peers.

In some cases, the "copycat" is not a younger sibling but the child of a parent who is either anorexic without acknowledging it or who urges the daughter to restrict her eating to an unhealthy degree. That was Caitlin's situation. Caitlin, now 22, was never a real binger. Just eating a normal meal is bingeing for her. She is an "exercisaholic." She keeps her weight under 100 pounds by relentless jogging, aerobics, and calisthenics. Caitlin's mother always made a point of preparing balanced meals for the family, but she rarely ate any of them herself. She viewed any added pounds on her size-6 figure with horror, and she served her daughter very small portions. "I grew up learning to be hungry," says Caitlin.

When an eating disorder becomes a family affair, it can be very hard to treat, since the family is providing support to continue the behavior rather than support in changing it. Be alert for evidence of collaboration and support of the eating disorder by any member of the family, and seek help.

It's All His Fault

Angie was brought up to believe her father was the most important person in the family. "He was almost like a god to us," she says. When Daddy got home from work, she and her mother and sisters were always cleaned up and waiting to greet him. Angie's father accepted this homage as his due. They were all remarkably well-mannered and considerate of one another—until Angie developed bulimia at age 16 and the family split down the middle.

The split isn't obvious. Nobody yells or slams doors. Loud, angry behavior has always been strictly forbidden. Angie's father is quietly burying himself in his law practice and takes no part in his daughter's treatment.

Angie's mother does take part in her therapy sessions, always carefully pointing out that her husband is "really a good man—it's just his way, he does his best." It's only in half-joking asides that she shows how hostile she really feels toward her husband: "He's a workaholic, you know. It's probably *his* fault she's this way" (with a conspiratorial smile at her daughter).

This attempt by Angie's mother to make her daughter take sides is only half-conscious, and it's destructive. A child can learn to adapt to parental disagreement, but to be asked to take sides with one parent against the other is very troubling.

This kind of demand is sometimes made on eating-disorder sufferers whose parents are divorced. Val's father, who lives in another state, often flew in to see her during her six-week hospitalization. He always showed her more gentleness and sympathy than could be mustered by Val's mother, who was close to the end of her rope after two years of Val's bad moods and manipulative behavior. He openly criticized the mother's strictness and told Val she'd be better off living with him.

A situation like this causes deep conflict, but the problem goes deeper than that. Typically, a victim of anorexia or bulimia has trouble recognizing and expressing her true feelings, especially such negative feelings as anger.

You as a parent can teach her how adults deal with anger. If you show your anger in indirect ways, like Angie's mother and Val's father, you are reinforcing her belief that such feelings are too awful to express openly. And make no mistake—children do pick up on underlying hostility between their parents, no matter how carefully it's buried. Getting help in facing such feelings and dealing with them constructively may be one of the most helpful things you can do for her.

Walking on Eggs

My eating disorder is the main focus of our family. If I come home from school for a weekend, it isn't me that's home—it's my eating disorder. I don't even exist. The stress and tension are so thick I have to cut my way from room to room.
Deirdre, 18

Much as they love her, Deirdre's parents and brother were relieved when she left for her freshman year of college. And, even though she's away, it's hard not to allow Deirdre's bulimia to rule their lives. They worry about her constantly. When she sounds unhappy over the telephone, the family feels unhappy.

Summers and holidays are the worst. When Deirdre isn't bingeing, she's dieting. As a result, she's always hungry and always on the verge of another binge. Her mother read somewhere that unexpressed anger and anxiety can trigger binges, so she's trying to manage their family life in such a way that Deirdre need never experience these feelings.

In this family, the simplest conversation has become a strain. After all, even a "how are you" can be interpreted as an under-handed way of asking her if she's throwing up. If she goes to the bathroom after a meal, everyone is afraid to say anything for fear of seeming to mistrust her. They hesitate to ask her to go swim-ming with them for fear Deirdre's anxiety over appearing in a swim suit (even at 102 pounds, she feels too fat) might set off a binge. On the other hand, they're afraid she'll be lonely and tempted to binge if they leave her alone. They "solved" the problem by not going swimming any more.

Fixing dinner is a daily dilemma. If the meal is especially tasty, it may be too tempting. If it's too blah, Deirdre's brother complains and drives his sister to her room in tears. It's easy to see why the whole family breathes a sigh of relief when Deirdre packs her bags and heads back to school.

Eating disorder sufferers aren't famous for being sweetly reason-able. Your daughter may make outrageous demands on the house-hold, with food as the usual issue. She may demand that the family change meal hours to accommodate her exercise schedule, order her parents to keep all sweets out of the house, or to prepare food without any butter or margarine. If she doesn't get her way, she may have a tantrum or a binge, or both. Between tantrums, she may be hostile and impossible to reason with. To an exhausted parent, giving in often seems to be the easiest way.

It's not the best way, though. Giving in hurts you, the family, and it particularly hurts the person with the eating disorder. You won't help your child by becoming a martyr to her disorder because your resentment is bound to seep through. And you won't help her by trying to spend all your time with her. In doing so, you may damage your relationship with your spouse, other children, and friends. You also won't give your child the encouragement she needs to take part in activities outside the family.

There is another reason your martyrdom won't help your child.

She is suffering from an eating disorder partly because she's never learned how to be good to herself, to take part in satisfying activities, form good friendships, and have fun. She may have to learn how to do all these things from the ground up. You are her most important teacher.

Give Yourself a Break

"I never had anybody to talk to!" This plaint of so many children with eating disorders nearly always fills parents with confusion and guilt. "What ever did we do to make her feel this way?" is the typical question.

Your child's eating disorder is not entirely your doing. The demanding schedules of most families today practically guarantees that time and energy for emotionally nourishing one another is in short supply. As David Elkind points out in *The Hurried Child*, the job of being a parent these days is complicated by a number of features that seldom crossed the minds of our grandparents.

For one thing, we're more afraid than ever before of violence in one form or another. We're more economically insecure, owing to world financial conditions, unemployment, and technological change. And we're more alone, thanks to our mobility and our record number of divorces.

We are loaded down with impossible expectations. We're taught that we should strive to be the best and to judge ourselves as successes or failures. We're taught that we should be "nice" all the time. And if we aren't as successful or as nice as we're taught to think we should be, we're taught to get rid of our bad feelings by jumping into the addictive cycle.

Many of us, strained to our limits, turn much of our energy and attention inward. We find it difficult to tune in to the deepest emotional needs of those around us—especially of those who, like most of those who suffer from eating disorders, aren't good at expressing their needs directly. Few parents of today get any relief from these demands in the form of the accessible aunts, uncles, and grandparents, in whom children of an earlier time could confide when their parents weren't there.

Short of packing up and moving to the Outer Hebrides, there is no way to make modern-day stresses go away. But one of the first steps in making them manageable is to learn to cope with two "killer" emotions—guilt and anger—as you watch your child struggle with her eating disorder.

Guilt: The Great Paralyzer

When I talk with parents about the uselessness of feeling guilty over past mistakes, I sometimes get the response: "But when you tell us not to feel guilty, aren't you telling us not to have a conscience? I mean, without guilt, wouldn't everybody forget about morals and do exactly as they please?"

I believe the answer to this question is that we often confuse two very different feelings—guilt and remorse. Remorse is feeling bad about a mistake you made in the past, and taking action to change your behavior. Remorse can be painful, but doesn't go on forever. It is focused on the present, where you can act and make a difference. Guilt, on the other hand, is less a way of learning from the past than being stuck in the present over a past event that is over and done with. In wasting your time and energy in feeling bad, you will have nothing left over for making changes. In that guilt can even be an excuse for not changing, it is an irresponsible emotion.

Another nasty feature of guilt is that it's contagious. Guilty people have a talent for making others feel guilty. Usually they are not even conscious of what they're doing because it has become such a familiar way of communicating.

The line "Do you have any idea how much you're hurting your mother by refusing to eat?" is an attempt to control by guilt. So is "Look at what you're doing to this family!" Your kids quickly learn that they can do the same thing to you: "If you cared anything about me, you wouldn't make me stay in this crummy hospital!"

Guilt can get to be a family game in which there are no winners. Watching out for guilty feelings and guilt-producing statements is a necessary first step toward more loving communication. If you find yourself brooding and feeling anxious over what happened in the past, stop. Stop yourself when you try to get members of your family to act in a certain way by appealing to their sensitive feelings, and don't allow yourself to be manipulated in this way by others. If your guilt seems overwhelming, get professional help. I wish I could recall the author of this useful reminder:

> Guilt is in the past:
> Anxiety is in the future.
> Where is your mind now?

Anger: A Case for Not Doing What Comes Naturally

> I never know what extra shopping I'll have to do for meals because I never know what's in the refrigerator. It's infuriating to come home after work and have to start dinner from scratch because all the leftovers are gone. It's frustrating, it's expensive, and it makes me feel rotten that I wasn't there for her when she felt she needed to binge. I can't help screaming at her sometimes.

It's likely that your child will pull some very irritating tricks in the course of her disorder. Anger is a natural response, and you certainly want to admit to it. You wouldn't want to hide your feelings under a pasted-on smile in the name of "peace." But owning up to your angry feelings doesn't mean you should unload them on your child. Ask yourself if your impulse to act will help. Scolding and diminishing a kid who already feels worthless won't help either of you.

Dealing with your anger constructively may well require some outside help. But you can start by understanding that your anger isn't caused directly by your child's behavior; it's caused by the way you interpret her behavior.

I had an appointment the other day to meet with a colleague at lunch. When the noon hour was almost over and he still hadn't shown up, I felt anxious—maybe he'd had an accident?—but not angry, even though I was pressed for time. My colleague is almost never late, and I was sure he couldn't help whatever had happened. On the other hand, if he made a habit of being late, I'd have thought: "Just like that inconsiderate jerk. Who does he think he is, anyhow? Doesn't he keep track of his appointments?"

When your child eats all the food or makes ridiculous demands on you, there's no good reason for you to sit there in silence and take it. You need to establish rules that will help her be responsible for her actions. Before you can do that, you will need to examine how your reaction to your child and her behavior is making you angry.

Chances are, you're saying something like, "Oh no, not again! She's just doing this to get even, that selfish little brat!" In other words, your immediate reaction is to interpret her behavior as malicious. This isn't usually the case. As we have seen, your daughter is either out of control or struggling to establish some control for herself. She has never figured out direct ways to express her needs and feelings. She's probably feeling some anger toward you, too, along with other feelings she doesn't fully understand. Her abuse of food (and, incidentally, of you) is a means of communication, a way of trying to tell you what she needs, not simple malice.

By focusing on selfishness or any other character trait you think is causing your child to do things you don't like, you naturally get angry at her, rather than focusing on the behavior that's causing the problem right now. In the case of the mother with the empty refrigerator and a family to feed, that's the immediate problem, not her daughter's weak moral character. A more useful response than screaming and yelling is to let her know she's eaten up the family dinner and that you need her help in solving the problem. Maybe she could go to the deli or help you fix something else for the family to eat.

This kind of approach to anger admittedly takes some work.

"Doing what comes naturally" is easier, and sometimes it is a relief to blow your top. But explosive anger won't feel good in the long run, and it can wreck a relationship if it becomes a habit. Most important, you aren't helping your child in the area where she needs help the most.

More than anything, she needs to feel that you are in control—otherwise, how can you give her the support she needs? She needs to see that you can have strong feelings without being overcome by them before she can learn to face up to her own strong feelings.

I don't want to drop the subject of anger without noting that there is such a thing as healthy anger. The father of 12-year-old Anna was angry when he talked to me on the telephone last week. He was angry not at Anna, but because the teacher at the dance studio had caught Anna throwing up again, because this had been going on for almost six months, because Anna was doing everything she could to resist treatment, and nothing was being done. Healthy anger, like healthy remorse, focuses on what is going on right now and what needs to be done about it. The anger is put to good use.

Checklist To Identify Unhealthy Coping Mechanisms

Your first step in coping with your child's eating disorder is to recognize unhealthy attempts at coping. If you find that you or other members of the family have taken "positions"—if your or their reactions to certain situations have become so predictable that you know in advance what the reaction will be—there's a good chance that you have taken on roles designed to keep things as they are. Here are some other signs of unhealthy coping approaches:

1. Has your anorexic or bulimic daughter's behavior become the focus of the family's attention?
2. Do your child's eating habits and food choices dominate your family's meals or schedule?

3. Are you or your spouse avoiding the problem by spending longer hours at work? Are you finding reasons to avoid taking part in your child's treatment?

4. Are you or other family members "walking on eggs" with one another?

5. Do you make guilt-producing statements to your child, such as "you are ruining the family" or "look how unhappy you're making your father"?

6. Do you often ask your child where she went and what she did?

7. Do you feel it is your responsibility to solve your child's problem?

8. Do you feel angry with your anorexic or bulimic child much of the time?

9. Do you often feel upset with yourself or your spouse for "causing" your child's eating disorder?

10. Have fighting or family squabbles become a way of life?

11. Have other members of the family begun dieting or changed their eating habits?

12. Has another youngster in the family become unusually quiet and withdrawn?

If these things are happening in your family, you're probably feeling scared, angry, and guilty, and your anorexic or bulimic daughter is feeling alone. You need help. In chapter 6, we'll talk about how to find it.

YOU'RE NOT ALONE:

Finding Professional Help

When we threatened to put Christine in the hospital if she didn't start eating, she seemed fine for a while. Then we found out she was gorging and vomiting in secret. We fought constantly—over food, friends, homework, name it. Whatever confidence I once had in myself as a parent was gone. We couldn't handle this alone.

Even after parents have acknowledged and accepted their child's eating disorder, seeking help is difficult. It's hard for a family to discuss their problems with a stranger who asks intimate questions and, in effect, takes over many parental functions. Helping your child get better may mean making changes within the family, and it's no secret that change doesn't come easy.

Parents may also be so intimidated by their daughter's tantrums and mood swings that they become afraid she will get worse if they insist she go for treatment. The fact is, most people with eating disorders have mixed feelings about getting help. Even while they're fiercely resisting the idea of seeing a medical doctor or psychotherapist, they are relieved that someone is there to take care of them.

Parents may believe they can't afford the fees for individual therapy (more on this later). Some think seeing a therapist is an admission that their child is emotionally sick. Or they may cling to the notion that problems serious enough to warrant professional help occur only among children who are neglected, abused, or economically deprived.

Even after the family has overcome these hurdles, they must find the kind of professional help that suits their needs. Specific treatment of eating disorders is a relatively new field, and you can't assume that every competent professional is familiar with this specialized treatment.

Not all physicians are aware of the emotional dynamics of anorexia and bulimia, and not all psychotherapists have the necessary knowledge of the physical effects. How, then, do you go about finding knowledgeable and caring help for your child and family?

Finding a Medical Doctor

To many people, checking out the qualifications of a medical doctor seems disrespectful, almost sacrilegious. However, there are ways to determine the doctor's ability to help your child without resorting to an unpleasant confrontation.

First, consider whether the physician is willing to sit down and talk with you about your child's disorder. You will have a lot of questions during the course of her treatment, and you want to be sure that these will be answered clearly. This is an emotionally trying time for you; the last thing you need is a doctor who won't give you the time of day.

Try to determine if the doctor is aware of the emotional issues involved. If the physician tells you to "make her eat" or to control her eating behavior in any way, you can be sure this doctor isn't experienced in working with those who suffer from eating disorders. You should also consider seeking other help if the doctor tells you your child will grow out of it or that it's just a fad she's trying out.

The doctor should advise a thorough physical examination and a complete blood analysis, called a *chem panel*. These are necessary and standard procedures for determining how far the disorder has progressed and what treatment is needed. If your child has been vomiting or abusing laxatives over any length of time, a blood analysis can reveal such problems as abnormally low sodium and potassium levels and abnormally high levels of liver enzymes. Your doctor should be willing to discuss the results with you in detail.

Following are some of the questions you should expect a medical doctor to ask you and your daughter:

1. How much has her weight changed over a specific length of time?
2. Has her menstrual period changed or stopped?
3. How has her eating behavior changed? Has she stopped eating? Is she eating only certain foods or restricting severely? What diets is she using? Is she eating much more than usual?
4. Is she using laxatives or diuretics?
5. How has her behavior changed? Does she have mood swings or tantrums? Is she withdrawn?

A competent physician will not want to treat your daughter's eating disorder alone, but should refer you to a mental-health practitioner experienced in eating-disorder therapy. The medical doctor doesn't step out of the picture, though. Continued monitoring of your daughter's physical condition may be necessary.

Finding a Therapist

You will want to take care in choosing a psychotherapist because your child and possibly your whole family will be working with this person over an extended period of time. There are two preliminary steps you might take in finding a therapist. One is to contact any of the eating-disorders associations listed in Appendix 3 for names of therapists and eating-disorders programs. While none of these organizations endorses specific therapists or programs, they take care to list only those with proper credentials and training.

You will find it easier to choose a therapist if you are aware of the various philosophies and methods of treatment. Descriptions of the most common approaches are provided in Appendix 2. Many of the books on the *Suggested Reading* list also examine the main types of treatment available, their goals, and their methods. This kind of information can help you ask the right questions and find the treatment that best meets your needs.

A prospective therapist should be thoroughly familiar with eating disorders. Whereas any competent therapist can help someone who is suffering from guilt, anger, anxiety, and low self-esteem, your child's physical state is also affecting her feelings. The therapist must be aware of that and be accustomed to working with medical doctors, dietitians, and hospital staff. Whether your child's disorder is in the beginning or advanced stage, it is extremely important that she get a complete physical assessment and blood analysis. If a therapist does not recommend this as standard treatment, find another therapist.

The person you choose to work with your child needs to relate to her as an individual. Beware of statements like "Your daughter is a bulimic." This equates her identity with her disorder. She is not "a bulimic," she is a complex, dynamic person with bulimia. This kind of labeling can be deadly because your daughter needs, above all, to find and develop her true identity.

The therapist also needs to be aware of your child's mixed feelings about getting well and her terror of giving up her familiar eating patterns. This kind of understanding takes more than credentials; it takes an appreciation of what you and your child are going through.

That is not to say you should judge a prospective therapist entirely on his or her manner. Certainly some personal warmth should come through, but a good therapist isn't necessarily one who talks a lot or makes an emotional display of concern. It's important that you feel reasonably comfortable with this person, though you can expect to feel a little suspicious and defensive for the first session or two. A good therapist will understand your feelings, as well as your child's.

You should also get a sense that the therapist accepts you and your family, as well as your child. Some therapists exclude the parents when they treat a child with an eating disorder. Sometimes this is desirable, especially in the case of a son or daughter who is about to leave home. Generally, though, it's more helpful to see the disorder as a family problem and to treat it as such.

It is not unheard of for a therapist to blame parents, particularly when the treatment isn't going well. Don't buy this. Blame is never productive. You shouldn't always expect the therapist to agree with you, though. Remember the object of the treatment is to solve a problem.

The therapist's job, in fact, is something like that of a management consultant who is hired to point out problems that members of the firm haven't seen because they're too close to the day-to-day operations. In other words, the therapist can help you get a broader view of how your family is operating. Some of your most deeply held beliefs may be challenged in the process. Be careful to distinguish helpful challenges from blame. If you are honest with yourself, you can usually tell one from the other.

It is also a good idea to find a therapist who is not completely sold on one approach to treatment. An eating disorder is complex and individuals respond to many different kinds of treatment. Your therapist should be flexible enough to adopt whatever procedures work for your child.

Remember that many factors can trigger and perpetuate an eating disorder: social influences, family problems, distorted thinking, poor self-esteem, biological issues, and the addictive cycle. It isn't helpful to focus on only one of these factors in treatment. For example, you should be wary of a therapist who considers only the biological aspect of eating disorders and treats them with medication alone, as well as one who considers only the psychological aspect and never recommends medication.

To locate a qualified therapist, contact one of the eating-disorders programs listed in Appendix 3 or on a national organization's referral list. Ask the program director to recommend someone. This will maximize your chances of finding a thoroughly experienced professional. Don't be shy about asking questions, no matter how highly qualified the therapist may be, and don't hesitate to interview more than one. Some questions you should ask include the following:

1. How long have you been treating patients with eating disorders?
2. Where did you receive your training in treating eating disorders?
3. What is your philosophy of treatment?
4. Do you recommend medication? What kind?
5. What is your fee?
6. Do you accept insurance? If so, how much of your fee will be covered?

You will want to discuss the therapist's fee on the first visit. Be aware that costs vary from one part of the country to another. In New York City, a psychologist's fee is approximately $125 per hour. In Los Angeles, psychologists typically charge $95 per hour. In my home state of Maryland, the average fee is $75 per hour. The hourly rate is generally lower in treatment centers: the fee for outpatient care in the program I work with is $50 per hour. Here are some recent average hourly fee scales (the therapy hour is generally 45 or 50 minutes):

- social worker: $40–$70
- psychotherapist: $40–$70
- psychologist: $65–$85
- psychiatrist: $70–$95

Don't let the fees scare you. Most insurance plans cover these services. If yours doesn't and you cannot afford the full amount, see if you can negotiate for a sliding scale or payment plan. Your community mental-health association may be able to provide some help here. Look in the Yellow Pages under Mental Health Services.

Individual Therapy

> Deep down every anorexic is convinced that her basic personality is defective, gross, not good enough, "the scum of the earth," and all her efforts are directed toward hiding the fatal flaw of her basic inadequacy. She is also convinced that the people around her, her family, friends, and the world at large, look at her with disapproving eyes, ready to pounce and to criticize her. . . . Therapy must help the patient to uncover the error of these convictions, to let her recognize that she has substance and worth of her own, and that she does not need the strained and stressful superstructure of an artificial ultra-perfection.[1]

The ups and downs of your child's therapy will make more sense to you if you understand what your therapist is trying to accomplish and some of the methods being used.

In general, a good therapist will decide on a procedure by working with the client. The overall goals will be to help your child improve her self-esteem and sense of competence, to resolve some of the underlying issues that have led to the eating disorder, and to establish normal eating behavior.

This is a tremendous task. To accomplish it, your daughter needs a person who can listen to her dark secrets without judging her or ordering her to change. The therapist says, in effect, "Let's look at what purpose the eating disorder has for you, then let's find some alternatives when you're ready to give it up."

Getting down to the basic issues is never easy. For one thing, most of the young women and men I counsel have simply never talked about their feelings in a direct, personal way before. They haven't learned to confront people and to express strong feelings toward them. One of the therapist's first tasks is to teach the patient to be comfortable in this one-on-one relationship, so she can feel safe talking about something more intimate than food and fat.

The patient also sees the therapist as an authority figure, which can be a problem. Even a nonauthoritarian therapist (and I wouldn't recommend any other kind) will threaten her fragile sense of control. She is likely to feel defensive at first, as though she's being interrogated. Or she may hide her feelings under a show of compliance. This isn't because she is being deceptive but because she has never learned to express her feelings directly. She may gain weight, as she knows she's expected to do, and then lose it all again at the first opportunity.

She's of two minds in another respect, too. Even though she feels out of control, she may also feel that she knows better than her therapist or her parents what's best for her. So she may smile and agree that she needs to eat and gain weight, but she's likely to feel, deep down, that she can rely only on her own judgment.

Getting in Touch With Feelings

One of the therapist's hardest jobs will be to help your child identify and express her feelings. This is difficult for a number of reasons. One is simply your child's lack of practice. In some cases, her relationships have been superficial—a fact that won't dawn on her until she has been in therapy for some time.

In addition, her focus has been outward for most of her life, trying to please others and figure out what they are thinking. Like most people with eating disorders, your daughter is often very perceptive of other people's feelings and completely unaware of her own deeply buried feelings. There is also a common belief among people with eating disorders that you won't be accepted and liked if you're not forever happy and smiling. The therapist's job is to find out what's behind that smiling face.

Another obstacle the therapist faces in getting at a patient's feelings is that she often dwells on problems with food and fat as a way of evading deeper issues. And, as we have seen, starvation causes increasingly distorted thinking. An anorexic's belief that she is on the brink of obesity gives her a "logical" reason for keeping up her iron self-discipline and makes her impossible to dissuade. When she changes her mind, it has to be her decision.

Learning to Be Assertive

Therapy, in the best sense, is education. Eating-disorders therapists regularly use teaching strategies to help troubled people over their fears, doubts, and obsessions. First, it is vital to help them feel confident that they can manage their lives and achieve their goals. Assertiveness training is often an important part of therapy.

One goal of assertiveness training is to encourage the client to think for herself. Decision making is often hard for people with eating disorders, not only because they always look to others for direction, but because their perfectionism causes them to agonize over every little choice. The therapist needs to help the client understand that not every decision is a matter of life or death and that there's rarely one "right" decision. For questions that aren't especially earth-shaking, like what to do in spare time, she will be asked to start making some independent choices. In more serious matters, the therapist will usually give her some guidance.

Assertiveness training will also help her identify her own needs and get them met without stepping on other people's rights. Often this will involve showing the client how to express anger. This usually causes some temporary turbulence in the family and makes parents feel she's getting worse instead of better, but it's a crucial part of the treatment process.

The thought that they deserve to satisfy their own needs seems almost revolutionary to many clients. But once they believe, they can learn healthy ways to confront people and get what they need. Role playing is a common technique for teaching these methods.

A New View of the Body

The client's belief that she is too fat springs from a kind of dream logic. Therapy can help your child see herself more realistically.

One technique is to show her what she looks like on videotape or in Polaroid photos. The tapes and photos help give her a new, more objective view of herself than the one she sees in the mirror. It's hard to be objective about what we see in the mirror, especially if we've spent hours studying our image, as many anorexics do.

The therapist or dietitian may also need to help the client change her mistaken beliefs about how food is absorbed by the body and what happens to make us gain weight. As soon as she begins to eat more or less normally again, or as soon as she cuts back on purging, a client often imagines that every bite she eats will make her gain weight. She needs to be reassured that only a small percentage of the food we eat gets turned into fat.

She also needs reassurance about the changes in her physical appearance as she begins to eat again. The complete lack of fat on her hips will seem to make her abdomen stick out, and she needs to know this is only temporary. Anorexics also sometimes think the loose flaps of skin on their upper arms are fat. In fact, these are caused by a lack of a normal padding of fat.

Though one important goal is to get her to see her body more realistically, the therapist (and parents, too) still needs to be very careful about commenting favorably on any weight gain. In the first place, such comments may be interpreted by the patient as a putdown ("They're not even seeing me—just my eating disorder").

Everyone concerned should understand that the weight gain doesn't seem like such great news to her if she's anorexic—it's scary, especially at first. It will be a long time, if ever, before she feels good about gaining weight. So don't expect the therapist to praise your youngster for putting on weight or to reprimand her for losing weight. That would only destroy whatever trust was established.

Although gaining weight or cutting down on bingeing and purging are generally signs that the patient is getting better, they are not the only goal of therapy. It is crucially important that your child go beyond this point and begin to feel comfortable with herself, or she will find something else to be obsessed with.

Group Therapy

Group therapy of one kind or another usually accompanies individual therapy. The major goal—getting beyond food and fat to the really important issues—is the same in both kinds of therapy. But working with a group has some additional aims and benefits.

People with eating disorders often cut themselves off from human contact because they feel that if others really knew them, and all the "horrible, disgusting" stuff they do, they would certainly reject them. It sometimes amazes them to learn that other people share their troubles and feelings. This makes their eating behavior seem less awful and something that can be safely shared.

Sharing is the first step toward accepting help and support from others—something sufferers of eating disorders find it extremely hard to do. Some of my clients have told me that their first experience of reaching out to someone else and asking for emotional support took place in group therapy.

Group members also learn to be real with each other. They learn that even if they say or do the "wrong" thing, it's okay. Their rigid black-and-white thinking doesn't apply here. The message they get in group is: "This is how you are. But here are some things you might want to do differently."

Besides learning to accept support and to accept themselves, members of psychotherapy groups quickly learn that they can't be as devious with one another as they can with their parents or even with their private therapist. Everyone there knows all the dodges and lies. They learn that they can confront one another and be confronted without feeling either rejected or devastated. This discovery makes honest friendship possible, and close ties often develop between group members. The ability to make close friends, in turn, makes each person feel better about herself.

There are obstacles to successful group therapy, too. Members sometimes challenge the rules that are needed to run the group effectively. Their distrust of other people can sabotage the therapy by making them afraid to open up. Their perfectionism may make them angry and impatient with group members who don't seem to be making progress. Or they may become competitive with one another over who is the "best" or the "worst" case in the group. Even so, most clients find their group to be a valuable part of their therapy program.

Psychotherapy groups, the kind we've been discussing, are conducted by professionals who generally charge a fee. Psychotherapy groups shouldn't be confused with support groups, which are usually free and often conducted by someone who has recovered from anorexia or bulimia, though some are led by professional counselors. Members can enter or leave a support group at any time, and the main activity is sharing experience and developing a support network. Like the psychotherapy groups, support groups cannot serve as a substitute for individual therapy. Also, they are not without some risks—a point we'll look at in chapter 8.

Family Therapy

Most therapists agree that the anorexic or bulimic patient will make better progress if the family is involved in therapy. Some believe the family therapist should not be the same professional treating the patient; others (myself included) think one therapist can work with everyone involved.

In either case, one of the main goals of family therapy is to help parents understand that they are not to blame for the eating disorder, but that they will almost certainly be involved in the recovery process.

The therapist can help the family support the child's therapy and help resolve conflicts within the family that interfere with treatment. In some cases, couples therapy will be recommended to help resolve conflict between the parents. To do a good job of supporting their child's treatment, families usually need to learn new and more useful ways of communicating.

The dynamics of family therapy might be compared, once again. to what happens when a management consultant is called in to help correct problems within an organization. The object is never to pin the blame on anyone, but to obtain each person's perception of what the problem is. Therapists can gain much insight from these family interviews, not all of it from what is spoken.

For example, therapists notice if one family member sits apart from the others or is unusually quiet. They will observe when one family member seems to speak for all the others, or when someone insists there really isn't any problem in the family at all—at least there were no problems before the daughter or sibling developed the eating disorder.

Some of the things the therapist particularly notes include the following:

- how the patient's behavior affects others in the family
- how the family's behavior affects the patient
- family communication patterns
- how conflicts are handled
- roles within the family
- family values, both spoken and unspoken
- family taboos

Family therapy reinforces individual therapy by encouraging the youngster to express long-pent-up feelings in a supportive environment. In one family therapy session, RuthAnne, the young woman who thought her sister was her parents' favorite, finally told her parents how abandoned and rejected she felt. The news came as a shock to her parents. They weren't aware of playing favorites and had no idea how RuthAnne felt. The progress of her treatment, which had seemed to be going nowhere, improved almost immediately afterward. Luckily, RuthAnne's parents reacted in an open-minded way, without getting defensive or overcome by guilt. Their positive attitude left them free to try out some new ways to interact within their family.

Parents vary quite a bit in their willingness to get involved in family therapy. They range from those who leave their child with the therapist with directions to "fix her" to those who are always on the telephone asking what more they can do to help. Neither extreme is very helpful to the child.

When parents don't choose to be involved in their youngster's therapy, I tell them, "Fine. That's your choice. But it is likely that your child will grow away from you."

Some parents come to the family sessions but don't really get involved. At one point, a 16-year-old client asked her father to leave the session if he couldn't stop joking around—his way of avoiding the pain of not being able to communicate with his daughter.

In the long run, the outcome of well-handled family therapy can be a happier marriage, happier kids, and a happier family. More than one parent has told me the eating disorder was a blessing in disguise.

Before things get better, though, they will temporarily get worse. Sometimes the child's disorder is a reaction to conflicts within the home that no one has yet been willing to face, let alone attempt to resolve. In such cases, the child's expression of what's bothering her can come as a bombshell. But if parents or other family members have the patience and courage to work it out, the results are likely to be worth the temporary uproar.

Drug Treatment

When medication is used to treat symptoms of an eating disorder, it's usually only one part of the treatment program. Because those with eating disorders often feel anxious and depressed, the medications most commonly used are antidepressants, which have proved helpful. In general, medications have been found more useful in treating the symptoms of bulimia than of anorexia.

Most researchers readily admit, though, that drug treatment of eating disorders is still in its infancy. Some people respond well to drugs and others don't. Medication can also be risky in some circumstances, or may have side effects that need to be carefully monitored and explained to the patient.

Naturally, care needs to be taken in prescribing any medications. Drugs must be administered by a psychiatrist or physician who is experienced in using them with those who suffer from eating disorders. Because it is not always possible to predict the effects of a drug, low doses are given initially and dosage levels are increased slowly.

Drugs aren't usually given to badly undernourished anorexics because no one knows how a drug may affect a starving person. Also, the symptoms of anorexic depression are usually helped by getting nutrition back to normal.

Hospitalization

Your daughter may need to be hospitalized if her eating disorder is too severe or persistent to be treated on an outpatient basis. If your doctor determines that she's medically unstable, she needs to be hospitalized immediately. The following conditions require immediate hospitalization for your child:

- Her weight is dangerously low. She has lost weight steadily and gained none back.
- Her blood chemistry is disturbed. Blood analysis shows low sodium and potassium levels, an electrolyte imbalance, or a starvation state.
- She is vomiting three or more times a day or the cycle of vomiting can't be interrupted on an outpatient basis.
- Her abuse of laxatives, diuretics, or weight-loss pills is extreme. (Some patients may be taking 30 or more laxatives a day.)
- She is abusing other substances, such as alcohol or drugs.
- Suicide is a possibility.

Patients who do not need immediate medical care may still need to be hospitalized if their eating disorder is severe enough to disrupt important aspects of their life. I look at all parts of a patient's life—family, school or work, social life, relationships, personality, and so on—and find out how many are affected by the disorder.

Let's say the parents of the anorexic or bulimic child feel desperate and don't know where to turn, her grades are dropping and she can't concentrate, and she's depressed. Her disorder is affecting three major areas of her life to the point of total disruption. Outpatient therapy can often help a patient get her life and symptoms under control, but this patient may need to be hospitalized for a time before the outpatient therapy can begin to be effective.

The best hospital is one that has a comprehensive eating-disorders program. However, since many hospitals across the country now have their own eating-disorders treatment program, choosing one can be perplexing. Anorexia Nervosa and Related Eating Disorders, Inc., offers these guidelines:

1. A good hospital program provides a supportive atmosphere for weight correction. Food is never used as a punishment.

2. The bingeing and purging behavior of bulimic patients is interrupted, breaking their addictive cycle, so their bodies can stabilize around normal eating patterns.

3. Weight gain or cessation of binge/purging is considered to be only one part of the treatment program.

4. Staff members give patients information about the physiology of starvation and binge/purging and about the emotional dynamics of anorexia and bulimia. Food myths are debunked.

5. Patients are encouraged to take part in healthy, noncompulsive exercise and group activities. Bed rest may be required at first.

6. Patients have frequent access to an individual therapist.

7. Family therapy sessions are provided, especially if the patient is younger than 16.

When Your Child Is Hospitalized

Your child may flatly reject the idea of hospitalization. Such thoughts as these may be going through her mind:

- If I start eating I won't be able to stop.
- I don't want to be out of control.
- I don't *feel* sick.
- If I give up my eating disorder I'll be just like every-body else.
- They'll force me to get fat.

When her weight loss or chemical imbalance is severe, though, it's your responsibility to get her into treatment whether she wants to or not. In presenting the idea to her (and you may want to do this with a therapist present), stick to facts and feelings: You lost 20 pounds, you're not eating, the doctor says your weight and blood pressure are dangerously low. We are all worried about you. You must get help. Period. Don't act apologetic, and don't hold the threat of hospitalization over her head to make her change her behavior.

The hospital experience is mixed for most kids, and it can be a trying time for parents, too. Fourteen-year-old Jessica was very cooperative when she first went into the hospital. After two weeks in the program she put on enough weight to earn weekend passes. But, though she still weighed only 90 pounds, her weight gain scared her.

"They're making me humongous," she lamented. "I eat that breakfast they give me, and it makes my stomach stick out. Then my whole day is shot!"

So Jessica began slipping food into the trash container when she thought no one was looking, and managing to throw up what she absolutely had to eat. As a result, she is now required to be on observation for two hours after every meal, and she hates it. "They have no faith in me," she grumbles.

Sarah, a 16-year-old patient, also complains about the "tyranny" of the hospital staff. Before her hospitalization, Sarah was used to doing 200 situps twice a day and running five miles every morning. Her dangerously low weight has made complete bed rest necessary until her body stabilizes and she starts gaining weight. But she's using all her ingenuity to get around this rule—doing secret leg raises under the sheets, making her bed several times a day, even vigorously brushing her hair by the hour until her hairbrush was finally taken away from her.

More often than not, though, the patients' hatred of the rules and their fear of losing control is offset by the positive aspects of hospitalization. Even Jessica admits that there are some advantages, like several girls on her floor offering to keep her company in her room—a kind of support she says she never experienced from her school friends. The staff also takes every opportunity to help build the patients' self-esteem by letting them know that they are likable and interesting.

Another advantage patients gain from their hospital stay is learning that they're not alone—that many other young people experience the same feelings and have tried the same painful ways to cope that they have.

They also begin to learn how to structure their time. Typically, sufferers of eating disorders have trouble knowing what to do with unstructured time. Their sense of who they are and what they want is generally unclear, and so periods of time that aren't filled with activities are scary. Just relaxing with a book, a television show, or doing nothing at all is something many of them have never experienced before, and they find it adds a new kind of enjoyment to their lives.

How can you help your daughter during her hospital stay? This is a question you will want to discuss with the therapist. Usually, you will be asked to take part in family therapy groups, where they are offered. You'll be encouraged to visit twice a week for an hour or so. You won't be allowed to bring food or to visit during mealtimes.

Health Insurance Coverage

The length of the hospital stay can range from less than a month to several weeks, and the expense can be a serious issue. However, most insurance companies cover the cost of inpatient hospital care of eating disorders. Typically, there is an up-front deductible, and the company will then pay 80 percent of the first $5,000 and 100 percent after that. Some companies have time limitations of thirty or forty-five days on their coverage. Some limit total coverage from $10,000 to $50,000.

However, some companies specifically state that they do not cover mental and nervous disorders of any kind. Since an eating disorder is considered both a mental and a physical disorder, it won't be covered by these companies. An occasional company flatly states that it doesn't cover eating disorders.

A therapist experienced in eating disorders can advise you in dealing with your insurance company. Hospital administrators can also be helpful. Insurance regulations will change as information about eating disorders becomes more widely known. The American Anorexia/Bulimia Association is lobbying and undertaking legal action to get improved insurance coverage.

Your part in your child's treatment is more important than it may seem to you. At times, you may feel pretty useless, but with strong support from parents and friends, as well as from the therapist, doctor, and hospital staff, your child will find it less painful to meet that hidden person within her and set off on the road to recovery.

Notes

1. Hilde Bruch, *The Golden Cage: The Enigma of Anorexia Nervosa* (Cambridge, MA: Harvard University Press, 1978), 144. Copyright © 1978 by the Presidents and Fellows of Harvard College. Reprinted with permission.

CHAPTER 7

TOWARD RESPONSIBILITY:
Authoritative Parenting

> I shoplifted binge food all last winter, and my folks pretended not to know about it. But one day I guess they had enough from their devious daughter. My dad sat me down and told me I had two weeks to clean up my act or they'd send me to a girl's school in New York. I was terrified. The words that stuck in my mind are, "We'll send you to a place where there is no love." I did clean up my act for awhile, so they didn't kick me out. But talk about feeling rejected—it was overwhelming!
>
> Heather, 17

Discussions about parents, children, and discipline usually focus on whether a parent should be strict or lenient, authoritarian or permissive. Most parents aren't completely comfortable with either approach.

Authoritarian parents are rigid and dictatorial. They feel they need to be in control at all times. This is an enormous energy drain, and also arouses all kinds of negative reactions in kids: defiance, anger, lying, bullying, people-pleasing, and withdrawal. The "let 'em know who's boss" approach may help keep a superficial order in the family, but the price for this kind of order is that children don't learn to be responsible for their own actions. They do as they're told because they have to. They learn to depend on external authority to run their lives rather than on inner controls.

The permissive approach—letting children have their own way, often at the parents' expense—is no better for kids or parents. Children who learn to pull their parents' strings by throwing tantrums or laying on guilt get an exaggerated idea of their importance in the universe. They learn to be selfish, inconsiderate, and demanding and also miss the chance to relate positively to others. Parents suffer by having to live with kids who have never developed inner control.

Parents generally adopt one of these two ineffective parenting styles because that's how their parents raised them. Since both styles make everyone involved pay a stiff price, many parents tend to swing back and forth between the two. Permissive parents may let things slide until matters become intolerable and then crack down. Authoritarian parents may periodically feel bad about using their power on the kids and swing over to a permissive position.

Parents of a child with an eating disorder are especially likely to swing from one position to the other because their fear, uncertainty, guilt, and anger make them lose faith in themselves as parents. Let's look first at how the authoritarian and permissive approaches can raise havoc in a home with an anorexic or bulimic child. Then we'll look at a more helpful approach.

Slamming the Door: Power Plays

Your child needs the chance to make choices. The communication patterns in an authoritarian home don't allow kids to make choices; instead, they cut off communication altogether. Authoritarian parents assert their own power and cause the child to withdraw or rebel. These unproductive communication habits are actually power plays. They say to the child: "We know better than you and expect you to do as we say. It's our job to take care of your problem; you can't take care of yourself." The underlying message is: "Your thoughts and feelings don't count, and we're not interested in hearing them."

More often than not, parents use power plays with the best of intentions. But that doesn't keep their kids from feeling put down, hostile, and helpless. Let's look at some of these parental power plays.

Do As I Say—Or Else

Twelve-year-old Laurie was in the first stage of anorexia. Every night her mother prepared a good meal, and every night Laurie ate a little less of it.

Finally, Laurie's father had enough. After all, he said to himself, who's in charge here? She's going to cut out this nonsense right now. "You eat everything on that plate," he shouted, "or you'll sit here all night until you do!"

Laurie's father feels frustrated and powerless. He cares about his daughter and he's afraid she's ruining her health. It would make more sense if he simply said so! But his feeling that he should be in control at all times gives him no choice but to assert his power and regain control.

The problem is that Laurie's father has put her in a position where she has no control. He's offered her no choices, which is enough to disturb any child. To an anorexic child, it's terrifying. He just fired the first shot in a war nobody can win.

Naturally, there are times when you must assert your authority as parents. However, you stand a better chance of gaining your child's cooperation if you offer her some choice and some power. Instead of issuing ultimatums, Laurie's father might have considered what he'd say to an adult friend under the same circumstance. He certainly wouldn't order her to sit in her chair until she cleaned up her plate. He'd be more likely to say something like, "You sure aren't eating much lately. I'm really getting worried about you. Can you tell me what's going on—what you're feeling that makes you not want to eat?"

This father wouldn't be giving up his authority if he spoke in this way to Laurie. He would simply be responding to the situation there, at the family table, rather than to the picture in his mind of how a parent should act. He'd be sharing his power with his daughter, and fostering a caring relationship with her.

I Know What's Best for You

Susan's mother recently turned to her daughter at the end of her therapy session and said, "Well, dear, what it comes down to is you're just going to have to use some willpower."

A helpful suggestion? Far from it. What Susan's mother is really saying to her is: "This is my responsibility. I know best." She has just taken from her daughter the thing she needs most—the responsibility to solve her own problem.

You probably know someone who specializes in handing out free advice, and you know how irritating it can be. "I wouldn't buy a car right now, if I were you." "Have you ever tried scheduling your time?" "Your problem is, you're not assertive enough." Comments like these feel like an attempt to exert power over you, and that's exactly what they are. Any time we try to "help" another person by telling them what they really ought to do, or by spouting facts at them, or by cross-examining them, we're saying "I know what's best for you."

Instead of advising her daughter to use some willpower (which she doesn't have at this point), Susan's mother could have given her some choice and some power. She might have said, for example, "How would you like to handle this, Susan? Since you vomited again today, what can we all do?"

Susan might not be able to come up with an answer, but she would know she is responsible for making the choice. Best of all, she would know her mother trusts her to make the choice.

It's All Your Fault

When Tommy's mother finally got home from work, she looked forward to a nice, warm shower before dinner. There was the leftover chicken from last night—all she had to do was fix a salad and reheat the rolls. If only Tommy didn't get to the chicken first. . . .

The kitchen looked like the scene of a food fight. Bones littered the counter. Mashed bread crumbs were stuck to the floor. Spilled milk was souring on the table. She rushed up the stairs and pounded on her son's door. "You filthy pig!" she wailed. "You are ruining this family!"

Tommy has been hard to live with, and his mother isn't a saint. Her reaction is perfectly understandable. The problem is that it's making matters worse for everyone. Tommy can't begin to take full responsibility for his actions until he learns to think more highly of himself than he now does. And his mother's harsh words won't help him achieve that goal. They can only make him feel even less lovable and capable than he already does.

What might Tommy's mother have done? First, she might have calmed down and responded to the situation at hand—her son ate up the family's dinner and left a mess in the kitchen. She might have simply presented those facts to Tommy and offered him a choice. "Tommy, you ate the chicken and rolls we were going to have for dinner tonight. The kitchen needs to be cleaned up before I can fix something else. What do you think we should do?"

There's no guarantee that Tommy will respond in a positive way. He may not respond at all. But he has received the kind of message that will help him make a healthy change, rather than one that can only make him worse. You will be amazed at the long-term results when you offer positive choices.

It is important to realize that parental power plays aren't always accompanied by harsh words. A child's feelings can be diminished in more subtle ways, often unintentionally, by denying her problem or telling her how she should feel about it. The message that comes through to children is "We don't want to hear what you have to say. We don't care how you feel."

You'll Feel Better Soon

Kara was bingeing on cookies after school and then vomiting. Her father had observed the signs—the crumbs and empty wrappers, the sour odor in the bathroom—but didn't know what to say to her. Maybe it was just a phase Kara was going though. Or maybe he was imagining things. Better let well enough alone.

One day Kara's father came home from work early with a sore throat. He found his daughter vomiting in the bathroom. She was pale and sweaty. "That's all right, Kara," her father said soothingly. "You'll feel better pretty soon."

This kind of "support" won't help Kara at all. Her father is simply denying that Kara is forming a dangerous habit, that she feels awful and needs help.

By denying the problem, Kara's father is trying to hang on to the myth of the perfect parent. Perfect parents don't have kids who binge on cookies and make themselves vomit; *their* children are happy and normal. Instead of considering his daughter, Kara's father is trying to convince himself that Kara will feel better soon so that he won't have to confront the obvious facts.

Kids can see through this kind of reassurance. When they hear don't worry about it, you'll be all right, or I know you'll feel better, kids know these messages actually mean, "I don't want to deal with this problem. I'm not interested. I'm afraid." A child can't begin to take responsibility for a problem if her parents won't even admit that it exists.

Kara's father might have acknowledged what was happening before his eyes: "This must be very hard on you. You're probably scared about what's happening. Why don't we go see the doctor as soon as possible and see what we can do." This response would make Kara feel that her father understands her and cares enough to offer real support.

You're Such a Pretty Girl

Melody examined herself long and critically in the hall mirror. She was wearing last summer's swimsuit and it was a bit snug. "I look like a hog in this thing," she said. "Look at those thighs. Pure blubber. Yech!"

"Mel, don't be silly," her mother replied from the kitchen. "You're such a pretty girl. You look nice in anything you wear."

Praising your child's physical appearance is risky. Since we are conditioned to judge our bodies against unrealistic standards, the young woman who is totally happy with her appearance is rare. Your praise is likely to be interpreted in ways you didn't intend. Your daughter may think you're dishing out praise as a consolation, or that you don't really know what looks good. She may think you don't understand or care how she feels. Still another danger is that your child may think an attractive appearance is the only way to earn your praise. She may go to dangerous lengths to assure herself of a steady supply of praise.

It would be better for Melody's mother to assure her that she loves her exactly as she is. "People come in all sizes," she might say, hugging her daughter. "You're wonderful just the way you are." No doubt Melody will still think her thighs are too fat, but she'll know her mother sees her as unique and lovable. She'll remember that and use it to help her build a more solid basis for self-acceptance than her appearance.

Stick to the Facts

Talking with your child about her weight or her eating behavior will be easier and more productive if you'll keep in mind the guidelines we've just discussed. One of the most important of these is sticking to the facts.

It's all too easy to become exasperated with your child and say things like: "Look what you're doing to the family! You never think about anybody but yourself, do you?" It's far more useful simply to point out that she ate all the family's snack food than to accuse her of being a selfish little monster. Better to tell her she's spending nearly all her time in her room than to say she doesn't give a darn about the family.

These points will help you avoid power plays and respond to your child in a positive way:

1. Talk with your child about what is happening here and now. Stick to the facts as you see them.
2. Tell your child in an assertive way that you're concerned about her health and happiness. Offer your support and love.
3. Give her the chance to make a choice about her health and the situation she's in.

Peace at any Price

Power plays won't help your child become more responsible and they won't ultimately help you get your needs met. But neither will letting her walk all over you. Most parents don't actually choose to do this, but they can fall into this position unintentionally.

Some parents are permissive because their own parents were too strict and they want to avoid making the same mistake. Or some may fear that any confrontation may set off a binge, tantrum, or depression. Still other parents may have tried to control their youngsters' behavior but discovered that the kids did as they pleased in spite of the power plays. For whatever reason, these parents gave up their authority and became doormats.

A child with an eating disorder doesn't want or need someone telling her what to do. However, she does need to feel that those around her are in control enough to care for her and help her to feel safe. To be nurturing takes a degree of strength and firmness. Let's look at some of the ways parents fail to use their strength for the sake of peace at any price.

It's the Least We Can Do

Erin has found that the family's normal meal hours interfere with her strict exercise schedule. She prefers to run four or five miles in the evening before dinner, so she's insisted that the family eat an hour later. Erin's demands are inconveniencing the family. The late dinner hour is making everybody irritable and late for their evening activities. Erin's mother has a standard answer to anyone who complains about this enforced change in their routine: "It's the least we can do for her. She needs all our help right now."

Parents naturally want to do everything in their power for a child in distress, but misplaced pity can do more harm than good. Erin should have some choice about what time she will eat (though I recommend that the family eat together at least two or three nights a week), but she doesn't have the right to tell the rest of the family when to eat.

Catering to this unreasonable demand won't help Erin resolve the problem that may have contributed to her disorder in the first place—her inability to have give-and-take relationships with other people.

By giving in to her demand, Erin's mother is conveying the message that Erin's wishes are more important than other people's. Because of her distorted thinking, Erin already feels that the whole world revolves around her and the issues that come first in her own life. An important part of the recovery process is letting her see that others have rights, too.

Another thing she needs to see is that her parents care enough about their own needs to ensure that they are satisfied. Demanding as she may be, she doesn't know how to do that herself. Her parents can be most helpful to her not by giving in to her every wish, but by showing her that they value their own needs and try to get them met by negotiating rather than by demanding.

The first time Erin asked the family to change their dinner hour to accommodate her running schedule, the most helpful response would have been: "Erin, I know you like to run right before dinner, but we won't change the time we eat because it's too inconvenient for the rest of us. This is our regular time for dinner, and we expect everybody to be there. Besides, your father and I wouldn't be able to get to our Spanish class on time if we change the dinner hour. You may want to think about changing the time you run or else cutting it a little short."

There's no point in losing your temper and telling your daughter how selfish and unreasonable she is. Value judgments like these won't teach her anything useful. Neither will sermons on being considerate of others. Your job is to help her correct her distorted thinking by responding to what is going on at the moment. All you need to do is explain that you can't give in to her demand and tell her why.

Feelings of pity may prompt you to make a number of other unhelpful sacrifices for your anorexic or bulimic child. You might spend a disproportionate amount of time with her, neglecting other relationships and activities. You might allow the family life to revolve around her. I know of one family who cut out the recreation they enjoyed because the teenage daughter was afraid of being seen in public in a swimming suit. I know another family whose meals are chaos because a bulimic child is allowed to "approve" their meal selections in advance.

Everybody involved in this useless sacrifice is bound to feel resentment, which can only strengthen the child's belief that she's a terrible, unlovable person. It also reinforces her eating disorder. She also needs to learn not to depend so much on you to meet all her needs. She needs to grow out of her passive, dependent attitude toward life. She must learn that the self-confidence she needs to make her own way in the world can come only when she takes risks and does things that are scary to her.

This is not to say that an anorexic or bulimic person should be pushed into activities before she's ready. In fact, she should never be pressured to change, because she needs those symptoms until she makes the decision to give them up. On the other hand, you don't want to make it too easy for her to continue her present behavior. And you certainly don't want to sacrifice everybody else's convenience and pleasure in the process.

It's Her Condition

Like most people with an eating disorder, Kelly has rigid ideas about "good" food and "bad" food. "Bad" foods include all sweets, snacks, oils, and "starchy stuff," and she gets very upset when she finds them in the house. One evening she came into the kitchen just as her father was browning some onions in butter.

"What are you doing?" she shrieked. "You know I can't eat butter in my food! You can all turn into fat, greasy pigs if you want to. I hate this place!" She threw her can of diet soda at her father's feet and stomped off into her bedroom.

Though Kelly has been in therapy for the past two months, she's still very anxious about controlling her weight and, incidentally, the people around her. Kelly's mood swings—her parents describe them as "unreal"—and her temper tantrums have become a regular feature of family life. Though her eating behavior is improving, much of her thinking is still distorted and irrational. Kelly's parents are reluctant to deal directly with her temper tantrums for fear of making her worse.

Kelly will gradually learn healthy ways to get her needs met without terrorizing her family. She'll also learn constructive ways to handle anger. In the meantime she needs to know that her parents won't put up with her abuse. Her father shouldn't say, "it's her condition" and let her tantrum go by without comment.

What he might do is go to her room and say, "Kelly, when you're not feeling so upset we can talk about this." Later, when she's calmed down, he might respond directly to Kelly's demands. He might say: "I'm afraid we won't cut out butter because the rest of us like it. We don't use a lot of fat because doctors say too much isn't good for our health. But a little butter improves the flavor of food, and I don't think the amount we use will hurt us. If you like, your mother and I can tell you which food is cooked in butter and you can just skip those."

This kind of response is useful in several ways. He's let Kelly know that the rest of the family has rights, too. He's pointed out that good health, *not weight control*, is what influences their food selection. And he's given his daughter the responsibility of making a choice.

Let's Try a Quick Fix

Temper tantrums and family fights are especially painful to parents who feel threatened by strong feelings. As a result, they may take a permissive or hands-off stance toward their bulimic or anorexic child in hopes that things will get better if they don't rock the boat.

Joni, 15, had been raiding the refrigerator after school for the last six months. She generally arrived home before her sister, who usually had sports practice after school, and long before her mother and dad got home from work. At first, Joni took care to leave enough food for dinner and clean up after herself. As she gradually lost control, she took whatever she could gobble, including frozen cookie dough and whole jars of peanut butter. Joni's sister complained angrily, but her mother said nothing. ("I never knew what to say to her," she told me later.) Instead, she started packing whatever she could of the family food supply into her car trunk and driving it to work with her.

What might first appear to be a creative solution to a tough problem was, in fact, an act of desperation. It was a quick fix based on the hope that if Joni were cut off from the food supply she'd stop bingeing and her eating disorder would disappear. Maybe loading and unloading groceries was a bit of a hassle, but anything was better, Joni's mother thought, than a frightening confrontation with an angry kid and no food for dinner. However, Joni is out of control and has reached the point where she needs to be hospitalized. Her problem won't go away by itself. The longer it goes untreated, the harder it will be to correct.

A child who regularly cleans out the refrigerator is infuriating to live with, but quick fixes—locking her out of the kitchen, locking the refrigerator door, not keeping food in the house—aren't helpful ways to correct the problem. For one thing, these feel like punishment to her, and do nothing to improve trust and communication in the family. Once she's in therapy, her counselor can suggest ways to handle problems that will help her become more responsible.

I sometimes recommend that a patient whose bingeing is not yet under control be required to spend her own money for her own food stash. It's understood that this food is hers alone to do with what she wants, and no one else in the family may touch it. A solution like this isn't just a quick fix. It saves the family food budget, but it also promotes the child's growth by giving her a choice.

How to Be an Authoritative Parent

No parent really wants to be a doormat or martyr, and very few really want to be dictators. But the alternative to these two approaches doesn't lie somewhere in between: it's an entirely different approach that we might call *authoritative parenting*.[1]

Authoritative parents are nothing like authoritarian parents, though the words look similar. Authoritative parents provide leadership, not dictatorship. They don't need to be the boss. They know that Father and Mother don't necessarily know best. They are supportive, but they look out for their own needs, too. They are real people.

They've managed to settle those deep-down quarrels with their own parents so they don't interfere with their desire to be good parents themselves. Whenever they need to take action with their kids, they ask themselves, "For whose benefit am I saying or doing this?" Not that they never do anything purely for their own benefit, but they know when they're doing it.

Authoritative parents know that conflict is a normal part of any relationship, and they don't let it throw them. One of the most important things a child with an eating disorder needs to learn is that conflict can be worked out without destroying the relationship—that it isn't necessary to swallow feelings for the sake of keeping peace or avoiding rejection.

A guide to authoritative parenting that I recommend is Dr. Thomas Gordon's highly successful *Parent Effectiveness Training*, listed in the *Suggested Reading* section of this book. Gordon teaches techniques for resolving major and minor conflicts with kids without shaming and alienating them. His books are available in most libraries and bookstores.

Gordon is opposed to the use of parental power because it doesn't allow children to make the choices they need to become responsible adults. He advocates a problem-solving approach in which parents and children work out their differences in a mutually satisfying way.

A word of caution, though. If your child has an eating disorder, especially one that has reached an advanced stage, she will need a lot of guidance to reach the point where she can resolve conflicts in the way Gordon recommends. If she's at an advanced stage of her disorder, she will not understand her own feelings or recognize her own best interests. One family I worked with tried the problem-solving approach with their anorexic daughter. This 65-pound young woman talked her parents into having a family conference to decide whether she should be hospitalized. She maneuvered the family into voting down the decision to send her to the hospital.

Your goal is to help your child take increasing responsibility for herself. In the meantime, the therapist will help ease her into responsible behavior as she becomes ready. It can't be forced.

How Can I Help?

Here are a few suggestions in response to the question parents often ask.

Leave Her Weight to the Therapist

Let the therapist negotiate with your child on issues of weight, food selection, and food abuse. As closely involved as you are with her, it's hard for you to see the problem clearly and objectively. You need an outsider to aid you in your efforts.

Remember that the real goal is not only to change your child's eating habits, but her belief system. You can help by *not* supporting her desire to be thin.

This may require you to examine some of your own beliefs and watch the kinds of remarks you make about your weight. It also means not letting your child pull you into long discussions about calories, diets, and body size. She is looking for someone to agree with her, and you don't want to do it. You can help her by opening up your thoughts and feelings to her and letting some fresh air into her distorted thought system.

Encourage Honesty

Has your daughter ever been afraid to tell you about something she did for fear of being punished? If so, you have an unwritten rule in your home that discourages honesty. Your child's evasiveness is a big stumbling block on her road to recovery. You can help her over it in two ways.

Confront her whenever you catch her lying, but do it gently. The object isn't to punish her. Fear and shame are at the root of her lies, and a punishing attitude on your part won't help matters any more than letting her get away with it.

Next, be open and honest about your own mistakes. Make it clear that yours is a home where it's okay to make mistakes. This is a point the therapist is trying to help your perfectionist child understand, and you can support that effort powerfully by your example.

You can encourage honesty by praising and trying to understand her attempts at being honest. If she reveals feelings in a family therapy session that surprise, hurt, or offend you, see this as progress. Show appreciation for her honesty. Help her to risk showing how she feels. In doing so, you will help her feel free to come to you with the truth when she's in trouble.

Offer Support

Most parents are more than willing to give their support. The only question is, how? Some actions that may feel like support to you may not feel that way to her.

Parents often try to support their anorexic or bulimic child's attempts to eat normally in ways that seem obtrusive to her. Remarks like "Are you sure you want that piece of cake?" and "Wouldn't you like another piece of chicken?" make her doubt her own judgment and create anger and guilt. She needs to feel your trust as she struggles to gain control over her eating. She needs authorities who can guide her but who can risk letting her make mistakes.

Support doesn't mean letting her depend on you too much. It doesn't mean staying home with her instead of attending an enjoyable social function that she feels anxious about going to. Fostering a dependency in which you try to fill all her needs and help her avoid doing anything difficult is an obstacle to her recovery. She needs encouragement to get on with her life.

Remember that there's no substitute for affection, verbal and physical. When you hug your daughter, squeeze her hand, or smile at her in a genuine way, you're speaking the language of the heart, and everyone flourishes on that. See chapter 9 for more discussion of how you can show support.

Work It Out

Make it a high priority to work out family miscommunication that gets in the way of her treatment. If you and your spouse are in conflict, this could have an adverse effect on her progress as well as make your own life miserable.

You and your partner do not have to agree on everything related to your youngster's treatment, and you certainly don't want to construct a phony united front for her benefit. You are separate people with your own feelings, and that's how you should relate to her. If your conflict is deep and bitter, though, you will want to consider getting some couples therapy.

Brothers and sisters often feel angry toward an anorexic or bulimic sibling for a number of reasons. She consumes more than her share of the family's time, attention, and money. She causes arguments and makes everyone feel bad. Sometimes she's just plain hard to get along with. Siblings may feel ashamed of being seen in public with her. Parents need to assume leadership in this situation and let her brothers and sisters know this is a family problem. Her condition should be explained to them, even though they may wish to have no part of it, which sometimes happens.

Recognize, though, that her brothers and sisters may feel a healthy kind of anger toward a kid who doesn't seem to care whether she gets healthy or not. Their anger may come from their concern for her. Often it's a sister or brother who discovers the disorder in the first place.

Give It Time

Recognize that no therapist has a short-term cure for an eating disorder (and if anyone makes that claim, run). Your child has mixed feelings about wanting to get better. There will be setbacks and periods when nothing seems to be happening.

Generally, it's a good idea to stick with it through the bad spots. The times when you or your child seem not to be getting along with the therapist are often the phases in which the treatment is moving into painful areas. Getting angry with the therapist may be a way to avoid the pain. Though this isn't always the case by any means, it's worth asking yourself some probing questions when you or your child hit the rough spots. However, if you or your daughter aren't getting along with the therapist, vocalize your concern. If you can't get the problem ironed out, ask for a consultation with another professional. You're not obligated to stick with a therapist you're not comfortable with. An ethical therapist will willingly recommend a colleague for a consultation. Such requests are common, especially when hospitalization is indicated.

What Would You Do?

Here are three situations often encountered by parents of children with eating disorders. Please read them and decide how you, as a parent, would respond to each one in an authoritative manner. Then I'll briefly discuss each one with you.

1. For the second time, you've discovered your daughter vomiting in the bathroom after a binge. You want to talk to her about it, but she goes straight to her room and shuts the door in your face. What would you do?

2. You've done the laundry and are putting your daughter's socks and underwear into her drawer. In doing so, you notice a box of laxatives hidden in the corner under some socks. Your daughter will be home from school in a few minutes. What will you say?

3. Your son has seemed very "down" lately. He's been going straight to his room when he gets home from school. He rarely sees friends any more, and he spends much of the weekend sleeping. You ask him what's wrong. He says, "Nobody likes me. They say I'm too fat." How will you respond?

1. Don't let the closed door prevent you from confronting her with what she's doing. Knock and ask her if you both could talk for a few minutes. State the facts and your concern for her. You might say something like, "Cathy, you've vomited twice this week. I'm very concerned about you. I notice you're eating less, too." Then offer your support. "If you're feeling bad, I want to help. But I can't help unless you talk with me."

It's now her turn to talk. If she doesn't choose to, there's nothing more you can do at this time. But you've expressed the message she needs to hear—that you recognize the problem, you're concerned, and you're ready to help.

2. Confront your daughter as soon as possible in a gentle, caring way. State the facts: "I was putting your socks away (you don't want to be accused of snooping), and I found this box of laxatives. Could you tell me why you're using these?" If she replies that she's been constipated, express your concern. Tell her you'd prefer that she see the family doctor if she's having trouble with constipation,

because laxatives can be harmful to the body. If she becomes angry at this, describe the facts as you see them: "I'm not sure why you are shouting at me if you're simply constipated."

That may be all the ground you can cover at this point, but you will have expressed your awareness and concern. Resist the temptation to cross-examine her. This will discourage her from discussing her problems with you.

3. Don't assume that he is imagining things. It's only too common for a kid to be rejected by schoolmates because of his weight, his clothes, or the neighborhood he lives in. It's important to help him deal with that unpleasant fact.

You might tell him, "There are some people who only think about how a person looks. But they aren't real friends. Real friends will like you just because you're who you are. There are a lot of people out there who'd like to have somebody like you for a friend."

Notice that you aren't minimizing his problem and using a power play by telling him not to be upset. And you aren't evading the issue. You're telling him this is how the world is sometimes, that you understand how he feels, and that you believe he's capable of solving his problem.

Being an authoritative parent may sound like a lot of effort on your part. It is. It may mean changing old communication habits to eliminate unconscious power plays. It may mean resisting the temptation to keep peace at any price. But as one mother said of her struggle to help her anorexic daughter: "Victory comes for us from small battles. We're all stronger from our struggle and the lessons we've learned."

Notes

1. For a discussion of authoritative versus authoritarian parenting, see Diane Baumrind, "Effects of Authoritative Parental Control on Child Behavior," *Child Development* 37, no. 3 (September 1966), 887–907.

CHAPTER 8

HELLO, SUNSHINE:

Recovering From an Eating Disorder

Just tell people the eating disorder isn't really the problem. The problem is not knowing how to live, not reaching out to people, keeping feelings inside. I'm feeling better now, because I know this is who I am. This is one of the things I do. I don't like it, but I'm learning to like me, anyhow.

Cindy, 19

"**W**ill my child ever fully recover from her eating disorder?" Parents often ask me this question, and it's hard to answer with a simple yes or no. To begin with, let's look at what most authorities on eating disorders mean by "full recovery":

- Normal eating. This means eating a variety of foods and enough calories to maintain a healthy body weight.
- Freedom from obsessions about weight and calories.
- Involvement in satisfying activities and relationships.
- A balanced life that includes recreation and relaxation.
- Long-range goals and realistic plans for reaching them.
- Ongoing work in resolving the deep personal issues— the need to be "special," perfectionism, fear of failure

131

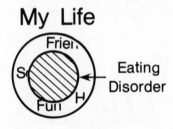

FIGURE 1

and rejection, low self-esteem, and the need for rigid control.

Reaching each of these goals is a process, maybe even a lifelong process, not a once-and-for-all achievement. There will be many ups and downs along the way. The problem with thinking in terms of full recovery is that it gives these perfectionism-prone people one more reason to think they failed if they don't meet the timetable they set for themselves.

The way I explain the recovery process to patients and their parents is to let them know, first of all, that life doesn't have to be perfect in order to be good. It is possible to live well and happily even with a serious problem. This is how it works.

Let's say your daughter's eating behavior is under control to the point where she isn't always thinking about food, and she enjoys some social activities. She is having trouble reducing some of the stresses in her life, and still binges and purges occasionally. The persistence of these old habits may be very hard for her to take. She may ask, "Why can't I get rid of the bulimia for once and for all?"

What I do is draw a picture to show that her task now is to concentrate on her growth, not on her problem. At one time, her eating disorder took up a huge chunk of her life (fig. 1). But now, I tell her, she has grown. She trusts more people, has new sources of enjoyment, good goals, a better relationship with her family, and improved self-esteem. So now her situation looks more like the one shown in figure 2.

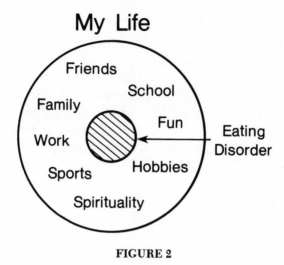

FIGURE 2

The problem is still there, but she is bigger and stronger, so the eating disorder takes up a much smaller portion of her life. The real task of therapy, as I see it, is not to take away the eating disorder but to help the patient grow to the point where she no longer needs it. The healthier she becomes, the less she needs her eating disorder.

At some point along the way, she'll say to herself—and mean it—"This is crazy stuff I'm doing." The eating disorder will begin to create a conflict for her. The conflict means growth. She will eventually feel more pain in keeping up her destructive eating behavior than in letting it go.

Rough Spots on the Road to Recovery

I've changed a lot since the time I weighed 70 pounds, but now I'm up against this hurdle I just can't seem to get over without somebody giving me a stepladder. I really wish I could make that last push by myself, but I can't seem to do it—not right now. *Lainie, 17*

It may be helpful to think of the recovery process not as getting over a disorder but as learning a new set of skills and mental habits.

Remember what you went through in learning how to swim, play tennis, or sail a boat? I remember that learning how to ski was a pretty ragged, sometimes painful, process for me. Five years ago I couldn't even stand up on skis; now I'm fairly competent. What happened during that five years is what happens in learning any demanding new skill, like recovering from an eating disorder. Let's compare the two processes:

Learning to Ski
1. I see others having fun skiing.
2. I decide that I want to learn to ski.
3. I decide to take lessons from a pro.
4. I struggle to learn the basics of skiing.
5. I make up my mind that I really *want* to ski.
6. I start skiing regularly and fall down a lot.
7. Skiing starts to be fun.
8. I feel motivated to keep practicing.
9. I go to an occasional brush-up class.

Learning to Live Without an Eating Disorder
1. She sees others who are not struggling with an eating disorder.
2. She decides she wants to recover.
3. She decides to get professional help.
4. She faces the struggle of giving up her addictive behavior.
5. She decides to continue therapy anyway.
6. She experiences the painful feelings she's been blocking and experiences relapse.
7. She begins to feel the pleasure of growth.
8. She keeps reinforcing her new attitudes and skills.
9. She continues working with a support group.

To master the difficult new skills needed to recover from an eating disorder, your daughter will need to overcome a series of hurdles. The first one is realizing that she has a problem which she might have the emotional strength to overcome—and deciding to get help with it.

I Need Help

This hurdle represents a tougher struggle than most of us who haven't had an eating disorder can begin to understand. It means that she will have to share with some total stranger a secret that has felt so shameful to her that not even her best friends know about it. Although until now she has used food or starvation as a handy anaesthetic for all her personal problems, she will have to face the almost unbearable feeling of emptiness that loss of the disorder always brings.

Once she's over that hurdle and has found help, the therapist's first job will be to get her eating behavior stabilized and her feelings about herself patched up to the point where she can start thinking about the real problems. Somewhere during this process she may need to be hospitalized.

The dilemma for many patients who reach this point is that they haven't really decided whether they want to get well. At times they do, at other times they're scared. They begin to see that getting well means changing their lives.

If a patient is bulimic, she is in constant fear that her bingeing and purging will be snatched away before she's ready to give them up. If she's anorexic, she's afraid the whole world is bent on making her fat. This is a risky time for her. She may decide not to cooperate, or she may decide to comply just to avoid conflict.

A potential danger during this period is that everyone concerned may put too much emphasis on her weight. Your daughter doesn't feel the way you, her therapist, and doctor do about weight gain and everyone needs to be sensitive to that fact.

It can be downright dangerous at this stage to say, "You look so much better now that you're not so thin." She is likely to interpret any favorable comment on her appearance to mean she's getting too fat. And she is likely to do almost anything to halt or reverse the weight gain.

Show approval and appreciation without referring to her personal appearance. If she tells you she's gained weight, ask her if that feels okay to her (unless it's obvious that she hates the whole idea), rather than applauding. Don't get drawn into lengthy discussions about her weight. Tell her you love her regardless of what she weighs, and let it go at that. You may want to bring up this issue in family therapy.

Another danger of placing too much emphasis on weight at the beginning stage of her treatment is that she'll get "cured" of the eating disorder without dealing with the underlying issues. If that happens, she may relapse into the old eating habits the next time she feels sad or lonely.

Concerned as you are about your daughter's total health, it's important to see weight gain and a return to normal eating as only *one* indication that she's getting better. Putting too much emphasis on it minimizes the deeper changes that have to take place, and will almost always arouse her resentment.

The Battle Within

Once she is over the first hurdle and her symptoms are stabilized, the next hurdle is deciding to cooperate fully with her therapist. She'll continue to explore her feelings and examine how she relates to other people, but she may not yet be totally committed to the recovery process. The difficulties she will encounter at this stage of her treatment spring from the continuing conflict within her: part of her wants to get better and the other part is still terrified, unconvinced that life would be better without her eating disorder. This journal entry by a young bulimic woman expresses how this conflict feels to her:

> The conflict is between my external self and my internal self. The external me tries to meet the expectations of society.

Society sets high standards: look pretty, be thin, be a compassionate and caring person at all times.

The internal me wants the freedom to express anger if I need to, to get my own needs met, instead of constantly trying to meet the needs of others. There is something about this conflict that just isn't right. I read once that bulimia is a scream of anguish, and I believe this is true. To fill the emptiness that results from the conflict, I use food. I use food to comfort me, to soothe my anger at people for not letting me be me.

Resolving this conflict can take months, even years, during which your daughter will continue working with her therapist and her group. She'll learn new ways of thinking and keep reinforcing the patterns she has already learned. She will grow to be more assertive and to challenge her self-doubts. She may keep a journal. She'll practice ways to stop the addictive cycle from running her life. During this therapy stage she may also still be obsessing over food, restricting her diet, or avoiding "fear foods." She may still be bingeing and purging, but will be far enough along in her recovery that she doesn't like this behavior. She is growing into a stronger person, beginning to like herself and appreciate her uniqueness. But she may not yet have had time to develop the personal resources she needs to give up the safety of her old, familiar habits.

This is an inner struggle, but it involves all the people around her. The best way you can help is by being open to change and resolving to grow with her by learning to satisfy your own needs. That doesn't mean selfishly ignoring her needs. It means learning the same skills she's learning so that you don't have to look to her recovery or her other accomplishments for your happiness. If you have the strength and resources to appreciate who you are, you'll make it easier for her to appreciate who she is.

Another way you can help your daughter through this stage of her treatment is to remember that continuation of her anorexic or bulimic behavior doesn't necessarily mean she isn't making progress. It means she has unmet needs that are keeping her stuck for the time being. The best thing you can do is understand these needs, not try to rush her. Let's look at some of them.

No Room for Error.   Your daughter's need for perfection can be a source of major trouble for her. It's hard for a perfectionist to accept those times during her treatment when nothing seems to be happening. She may use such apparent lack of progress to convince you she shouldn't be in treatment. Although she needs time to consolidate new ways of thinking and feeling, that's not easy for her to accept.

Her perfectionism may also make her demand flawless performance of herself. As she starts feeling better, she'll notice some good changes, but one binge can make her feel worse than ever. She'll feel like a rotten person, a total failure.

Your daughter (and you) should realize that when she wants to binge, she'll binge, and there may be nothing she can do at this point to stop it. As her binges become less frequent, she needs to give herself credit for the progress she's made, not be hard on herself for occasional lapses.

You can encourage her to think in this positive new way by seeing periodic setbacks as a normal part of the treatment process rather than a cause for worry. Be aware of perfectionist tendencies in yourself and consider whether they are necessary. Set an example by showing satisfaction over your own less than perfect performances and being gentle with yourself when you make a mistake.

Avoiding the Issue.   Your daughter needs to feel in control. The personal issues raised in therapy will feel uncontrollable to her, and she'll find ways to avoid facing them.

She may direct the discussion in therapy toward food, weight, and other external problems as one way of escaping strong feelings. One 18-year-old bulimic recently admitted to me that she was pushing aside the painful, gut-level feelings that were beginning to surface by intellectualizing them. She knew her task at this point was to feel her feelings and act on them, not merely talk about them.

There are other ways to sidestep the real issues. Some young women keep on trying to fill the old "perfect me" role they think is expected of them. No matter how terrible they feel, they do their best to appear happy and self-sufficient. "How are you?" I recently asked a young bulimic woman who had threatened suicide the week before. "Just great!" she replied with a big smile.

As a parent you can help by showing your child that it's okay to wear the kind of face that's appropriate to your feelings. If you're sad, let the sadness show and don't apologize. Realize that this cultural taboo against showing the so-called negative feelings is actually a taboo against feeling, and that learning to express those feelings is one of the hardest jobs she faces on her road to recovery.

Finding Substitutes.   Remember I mentioned earlier that people with eating disorders often feel there's a void in their life? They feel empty because they're removed from their own feelings and must rely on external cues to let them know how to act. They don't have a clear sense of who they are, how they feel, or what they want.

For this reason, sufferers of eating disorders typically have a hard time knowing what to do with themselves when they're alone and have free time. They feel lost, almost like nonpersons, when there's no outer activity or person to respond to. A good treatment program will help them use unstructured time in satisfying ways, but it may continue to be a problem. Your daughter has to learn how to resist the need to substitute external time-fillers for thinking about who she is and what she really wants.

If she's a student, she may be tempted to take on a heavy work schedule during school vacations so she won't have to cope with free time. In fact, workaholism can easily become a substitute for an eating disorder. "My sense of balance is missing," said one client who held two waitressing jobs during her summer vacation. "How do you keep from making some one thing all-important?"

It's all too common for people with eating disorders to make something else all-important as long as their feelings are blocked. Their sense of emptiness makes them reach for whatever filler looks most promising, whether it's food, work, sex, drugs, consumer goods, or winning tennis trophies. When any of these is used in a driven way, as a substitute for feelings, it can only do more damage to her self-esteem.

Another substitute for feelings is the helper role many sufferers of eating disorders take on themselves. Your daughter may, for example, want to do all the family shopping and cooking. These are ways to deny her own need to be nurtured and to help her feel in control. Taking on a helper role is not a sign of progress, and you won't want to encourage it. Do not encourage any kind of activity that looks like a substitute for feeling.

Learning to Live Again

No one I know of is glad she suffered from an eating disorder, but recovered patients often say they might never have found themselves if their dangerous condition hadn't forced them to look within. Learning to live again is how they describe their recovery.

They learn to live again by starting to reach out to other people instead of always trying to appear self-sufficient. They find healthy alternatives to addictive behavior. They use food and exercise to enhance their life instead of ruling it. In short, they start leading a balanced life.

Learning to reach out to others, in particular, is a turning point in the lives of these young people. In many cases, they've always been praised for being strong and independent, but they never felt strong and independent. Instead, they lived in fear of getting close enough to anyone to reveal the boring, weak-kneed people that they imagined themselves to be.

It's not only parents who may make children feel they have to act more strong and independent than they feel. Our whole society places an unhealthy emphasis on self-sufficiency. Many of us don't learn that it's acceptable to give and get help until trouble strikes and we're forced to accept help from others.

Generally it is in group therapy that people with eating disorders make this discovery. They often exchange telephone numbers and call one another when they need support. This is very hard for them to do, but it gradually teaches them that they can reach out and be accepted. Sharing feelings with fellow sufferers feels safe, and it paves the way to a growing network of people they can trust and communicate with.

Learning to Be Me

As your daughter learns to reach out to others, she'll learn to relate to people in new ways. She has learned in group therapy what it's like to express her feelings and be real with people, and she will no longer be contented with superficial relationships. She may decide that some of her friends aren't friends at all, and seek more satisfying companions. This is how one client put it:

> Now I look at school friends and say, "What are they really looking at? My hair? My face?" I know a lot of them aren't really seeing my personality. But now I have a feel for who's like that and who isn't. And I'm making more of an effort to be myself.

Relationships with parents and family will change, too. A typical comment is, "They used to talk about not very important stuff, like 'How was school?' and 'Did you clean your room?' But now my parents are more open. They talk to me like a friend." This new openness within the family is a major step toward recovery.

Learning to Live With Food

After your child's disorder is addressed, she'll be encouraged to start a meal plan and begin normal eating patterns as soon as possible, whether she is treated in the hospital or as an outpatient. Normally a dietitian does the nutrition counseling. Make sure that this person is a Registered Dietitian, a professional accredited by the American Dietetic Association.

The objective of nutrition counseling is to help your daughter develop a moderate attitude toward food and to make a habit of healthful eating. One of the first steps in this process is to help her overcome her distorted attitudes toward food. People with eating disorders are extremely anxious about eating foods they believe to be fattening—beef, bread and other carbohydrates, and sweets. They need to be convinced that the calories in these foods have no greater effect on their weight than the calories in their "good" foods—the fruits, vegetables, and low-calorie items. In the program I am involved in, our dietitian stresses to patients that there are no bad foods. Bulimic patients aren't asked to eat any of their "fear foods" at first because of the danger that they'll binge on them. But when we feel they can handle them, we encourage them to start adding these foods to their diets a little at a time.

We also encourage patients to eat normal food portions. They nearly always overestimate the amount they're eating and are usually amazed to learn how much food is actually needed to make them gain weight. We try to encourage compulsive calorie counters to start thinking in terms of their energy needs rather than calories.

We let patients know about the changes that will take place in their bodies as they start to eat normally. Their initial weight gain may be alarmingly rapid if they're dehydrated or have stopped vomiting or using laxatives. They need reassurance that they won't continue to gain at this rate, and that their body will adjust to normal eating. Our clients usually also experience some bloating, constipation, and other discomforts as their body gets used to being fed normally again. We try to help them be more relaxed in general about food, but until normal eating becomes part of their life, the diet plan we impose may be fairly rigid in terms of food types, portions, and meal times. Patients may be asked to eat at regular times each day and to consume a certain number of calories. Since their idea of what a normal portion is may be way off, I sometimes take patients to lunch to help them see that the serving sizes they're allowing themselves are still very skimpy.

Their fears are hard to overcome, though, and patients often find ways to "cheat." They may still overeat at times and then try to make up for it by skipping or limiting meals. They may drink a lot of water before their checkup to make the therapist think they're gaining more weight than they really are. They may continue to hoard or throw away food even after they've started to eat normally.

Holidays and birthdays are a trial for recovering bulimics and anorexics, times when family support and understanding are especially needed. If your daughter is in treatment, the dietitian can help you plan holiday meals without all those rich goodies that are a problem for most bulimics. Maybe you can even find ways to deemphasize food at these times.

Your daughter will learn a whole new set of habits and attitudes that will help her live more comfortably with food. She will learn

- The basic food groups and essential nutrition
- To see calories as energy units, not as fat-makers
- To recognize hunger and to eat at proper times
- To prepare herself mentally for difficult meals
- To be honest with herself and others about food intake
- To develop interests and activities outside of food

Alternatives to Addiction

Willpower alone never stopped anybody from bingeing. Controlling that addictive eating behavior takes a combination of personal growth and techniques that your daughter can make a part of her daily routine.

I tell patients that a binge doesn't start until they take action. It's important for them to break the cycle at the very beginning, before they walk into the kitchen or the donut shop, toss the food into the garbage, or fix that lettuce leaf and tomato slice for lunch. Before they act, they need to explore what they are feeling and ask, "What will I do about this?" It's tempting to binge or choose some other addictive action—smoking, drinking, buying clothes, or exercising compulsively. But it's always possible to do something more constructive. The choice is always there.

One technique I recommend as an alternative to addictive behavior is called the fishbowl. I ask patients to sit down when they're feeling good, and think about the things they really enjoy doing, and write these activities down on slips of paper and put them into a bowl or a box. When the person feels uptight, anxious, and about to binge, she chooses a slip of paper out of the bowl and does what it says. In this way, she interrupts the addictive cycle at the very beginning.

The success of this technique depends a lot on the kinds of activities chosen. To be effective, they should be human, emotional experiences that give a real lift—like nature, art, or being with a good friend. I don't rule out the small experiences that make us feel good, like taking a warm bath or buying a bunch of flowers, but they should not be linked to substances of any kind, like food or alcohol.

Another alternative to bingeing or starving is to write in a journal. A journal isn't the same as a diary. It is not a record of activities, but of emotions. A journal gives people an outlet for their feelings, both happy and unhappy, and also helps them see what triggers these feelings. I suggest to patients that they try writing in their journals for a few minutes when they feel like bingeing. The writing may relieve their need to binge, or, if they're not ready to give up bingeing, it may not. It's important that they accept themselves as they are now, and to take one step at a time.

Support Groups

I strongly recommend that patients continue working with a support or after-care group for a year after discontinuing individual therapy, and that the group be under the guidance of a trained counselor. Some excellent self-help groups led by nonprofessionals have been formed in the last few years, and many people have been helped by them. But they're not for everyone.

Anorexia Nervosa and Related Eating Disorders, Inc. (ANRED), suggests that young teens or those whose eating disorder has just begun steer clear of support groups led by laypersons. I agree. The group may teach them ways of abusing food that they hadn't thought of yet, or encourage them to take a kind of perverse pride in labeling themselves as "an anorexic" or "a bulimic," and make it all the harder for them to develop a healthy identity. People with serious emotional disturbances shouldn't be in a self-help group, either. This kind of group experience could be harmful to themselves and others.

Even if your daughter doesn't fit any of these categories, you should be aware of other kinds of problems that can arise in a group led by a layperson. Nonconstructive or hurtful comments may be made in the heat of discussion, and no one is there who is experienced in handling them. Besides, group members are often skilled in playing competitive games like "who's the thinnest?" and "who's the worst binger?" It takes an experienced leader to steer the participants out of these potentially harmful blind alleys.

You and Your Child's Recovery

In addition to her inner struggle, your child will have one other problem to cope with. There will be the friends, relatives, or teachers who make insensitive, well-meant comments like "You look so much better now that you're not so skinny." They don't understand what violently mixed feelings she has about her weight gain.

You can't follow your daughter around and protect her against rude or well-meaning remarks. All you can do is let her know that some people will make such remarks, and that the appropriate response is to say "thanks" and forget it. Or she may want to educate them herself. Either way, learning to handle other people's shortcomings is a part of her growth process.

If she's still in elementary school, you might ask her how she would feel about going with you to explain her condition to her teacher, especially if she's going to be hospitalized and out of school for some time. The chances are that a high school kid will veto this plan, but many high school personnel are well aware of eating disorders and know how to respond to students who suffer from them.

Though you can't take away the pain and you cannot make recovery happen, you will play a part in letting it happen by offering your support when it's needed, by sharing your power with your child, by giving yourself credit for doing your best at a hard job, and by growing along with your daughter.

This is how one mother expressed the way she felt about her daughter's recovery process:

Being the Mother of a Daughter With Anorexia Nervosa Means . . .

Forcing yourself to face what [anorexia] really is and means, and to absorb the shock that it is actually happening to *your* child;

Enduring the agony of watching your lovely daughter, to whom you have always felt so close, slowly waste away, withdraw, and lose touch with reality;

Realizing that using logic, bribery, force, or punishment is merely a waste of energy and emotion;

Accepting anger, helplessness, despair, and total frustration as a way of life, but somehow managing to maintain control when you want to explode and/or scream—or worse;

Regretting that you ever entertained the notion that it might be nice to have a daughter who enjoyed cooking!

Forgetting what it is like to regard food normally, feeling strange around those who *do*, and noticing how it is affecting your own eating and buying habits;

Wishing that there were some convenient substitute for food and that the word "calorie" had never been invented!

Learning to live only one day—or hour—at a time;

Sensing that you are indeed losing control of your *own* life;

Feeling guilty and somehow responsible for what has happened—yet not seeing how the past could or should have been different;

Discovering the true meaning of the old adage: "The road to Hell is paved with good intentions";

Accepting the obvious fact that because you have apparently "failed" as a mother (when you always thought you were doing so well!), you must now rely on professional help to raise your child—and resenting it;

Being sometimes totally overwhelmed by the irony and injustice of it all;

Burying goals and plans for the future which had seemed so possible and secure;

Knowing what a broken heart feels like;

Desperately resisting becoming bitter and cynical;

Wondering if the nightmare will ever end;

Needing, seeking—and finding—God's strength and guidance;

Gaining greater self-knowledge, and observing other family members doing the same;

Realizing more and more that underneath your daughter's torment and confusion is a very clever, self-centered, and selfish individual;

Learning to recognize the many forms of an anorexic's subtle manipulations, striving to stay one jump ahead of them, and squirming when you see others "taken in";

Struggling to achieve and to maintain the best balance as you constantly walk the tightrope between sympathy and firmness;

Having the courage to allow—and even to force—your daughter to make her own decisions (especially about food), realizing that you can help most by not seeming to help at all;

Listening, listening—over and over again—to her resolutions to achieve control, praying that *this* time she'll succeed—but being ready to listen again when/if she doesn't;

Being patient, no matter how difficult it is—knowing that experience is the best teacher and time the greatest healer;

Measuring progress only by inches, and by comparing what *is* to what *was*—not to what *might be*;

Above all . . . never giving up hope, and always having faith, that it will end—and that your daughter will enter adulthood, and live the many years ahead of her, with far more self-knowledge, genuine feelings, compassion, and strength than ever would have been possible had she remained that "perfect child."[1]

Notes

1. Nicki Meyer, *Being the Mother of a Daughter with Anorexia Nervosa Means . . .* Originally published in the newsletter of Anorexia Nervosa and Related Eating Disorders, Inc. (Eugene, OR: ANRED, Inc., 1982), 3, no. 4:3. Reprinted with permission.

CHAPTER 9

THE OPEN DOOR:

Communication in Healthy Families

My parents are really nice people. I mean, they never fight like some parents do. Even when I know they're feeling bad, they'll smile and act cheerful. They worry about us all the time, and I know they want the best for us. But I just can't talk to them. Not now. They'd be so disappointed in me.

Kelly, 16

You've seen them being wise and strong, week after week, on "The Waltons" and "Little House on the Prairie." More recently, you've seen their pictures in the magazines—parents who managed to rear six fabulously successful children during time off from their 80-hour work weeks. They represent an ideal that's lodged in the unconscious mind of nearly every parent in our society. It's called the myth of the perfect parent, and it's the sworn enemy of good family communication.

The idea that a parent should be all-wise and all-powerful at all times weighs us down with collective guilt. You'd never catch the Waltons doing some of the things real parents do—nagging, losing control, or having to rush off to work when their child needs help with math homework. The Waltons' harmonious lives are made up of funny, heartwarming episodes.

On the other hand, the Waltons never faced the challenge of living with a chronically hostile or depressed teenager. The myth of the perfect parent denies that everyday problems like troubled kids even exist. It encourages you to cover up problems with politeness and a happy face. It suggests that you can "have it all"— perfect children, a perfect marriage, and a perfect career. Since there are no perfect people walking the earth today, the myth prevents you from meeting the real needs of real people, starting with your own.

The Self-Nurturing Parent

Personal needs can't be denied. All of us need our own sources of satisfaction: we need to feel that we're using our talents productively; that we have the support of friends; we need fun. Most of all, we need to feel that our lives have meaning.

When we're taking care of our personal needs, we can let our kids set their own goals. We can accept them as they are and not insist that they fulfill our ideals. When we have our own sources of satisfaction, we can talk and listen to children without the static of our frustrated wishes and unspoken expectations getting in the way.

If we don't have these sources of satisfaction in our own lives, we'll look for them in other people—all too likely, in our children. As a result, we may set unrealistic standards for their behavior or appearance. We may even pressure them to fulfill our own buried dreams.

Here are eight questions to help you determine how well you're meeting your own deepest needs. Find a time when you won't be disturbed. Think them through carefully and answer them honestly.

1. Do you have work or a creative pursuit that gives you
a sense of personal achievement?

2. Can you have fun with activities in which you're not accomplished?

3. Do you feel safe just being yourself?

4. Do you have the emotional support of close friends?

5. Are you taking active measures to help you cope with daily stress (meditation, prayer, exercise, etc.)?

6. Is your life reasonably well organized?

7. Do you have a philosophy or belief that gives your life meaning?

8. Have you forgiven your parents and yourself for past mistakes?

If you answered "no" to any of these questions, please consider ways to be kinder to yourself and to your family. More than anything else, your children need the model of a balanced, satisfying life. This is especially true today, with phony values being pitched at them from every direction. Kids need to see their parents forging a life for themselves, not just surviving from day to day.

Learning to nurture yourself may be the most important step you can take in helping a child who is battling an eating disorder. These are people who have no idea how to nurture themselves. As we've seen, an anorexic's biggest pleasure in life may be preparing delicious meals for others to enjoy. She needs to learn how to find satisfaction from within herself, and she can learn that most easily from you.

Your "Care Package"

Some child-care manuals help perpetuate the myth of the perfect parent by assuming that parents are more patient and understanding than they actually feel much of the time. It's taken for granted that they'll act in a consistently wise, mature manner.

Good parenting comes in many styles. Your primary gift to your child is your genuine concern for her health and happiness. But your gift can come in a variety of wrappings. It can be meticulously wrapped and tied up with colored ribbons, but no one will turn it down if it's bundled up in crumpled newspaper. The important thing is that the gift is inside there for kids to see and feel.

I'm thinking of a large, noisy family that lived in the neighborhood where I grew up. I'll call them the Shermans. Mr. Sherman, a sales representative, was on the road most of the time; Mrs. Sherman was deeply involved in local party politics. Their four sons were so involved in auto mechanics that the street in front of their home looked like a wrecking yard. Their house was a mess, and Shermans were rushing in and out of it all day and half the night. Sometimes they rocked the neighborhood with shrill family quarrels, followed by the screech of a teenager's tires.

The Shermans' communication skills could have stood some improvement. But Sid and Mary Sherman cared about their kids and let them know it. They were openly affectionate. They welcomed their children's friends into their home. They went camping and skiing together. Their "care package" came in a messy wrapping, but the kids accepted it anyway.

The key words here are "they let them know it." You who are reading this know you care for your kids and take it for granted they know it. In fact, they may not. Many parents shy away from intimacy with their children. They feel awkward about expressing their deepest feelings to them. This, too, is partly the result of the perfect-parent myth. Many times parents think they're letting the kids down if they don't always appear to be in control, powerful, and all-knowing.

Very young children need to believe their parents know everything. I was 15 before I discovered otherwise. But my parents had always shared their feelings with me, so there were real people there to fill the gap when it dawned on me that they weren't quite perfect after all. And I was willing to settle for real people who cared for me.

How do parents let their kids know they care? We'll look at some of the ways. They may feel awkward to you at first, and you may not come across like the Waltons. But remember, your kids will value your gift no matter how it's wrapped.

Being There

Marian teaches history at the local university. Her hours are flexible, so she's there to greet her 12-year-old daughter, Carla, when she gets home from school. Usually Marian is hard at work on her research project, but she encourages Carla to talk about her day. Marian congratulates herself on being able to write while her daughter chats about teachers, boys, and the new shoes she needs. That's why Marian was so astonished when Carla suddenly burst into tears one day and stomped out of the room, shouting, "You're not even interested! All you care about is your old school work!"

No parent can drop everything and offer complete attention every time a child wants to talk. There are many other demands on your time, and children need to know that. On the other hand, your readiness to give them your undivided attention at times is a powerful way to show you care for them.

When you stop to think about it, your relationship with your kids is basically no different from your relationship with adult friends. It's closer, of course, and you have responsibilities to your children that aren't present in these other relationships. But the style of communication needn't be radically different. If a friend drops by your office with a personal problem he wants to discuss, you probably won't keep writing your memo or straighten out your desk drawer. You won't suddenly remember an errand and rush out the door. Certainly you wouldn't tell your troubled friend he'll grow out of it.

You would probably pay attention or, if you had to finish that memo right now, ask him to come back in an hour when you could take time to listen to him. Or maybe you'd arrange to have coffee with him tomorrow morning. In whichever case, you'd save yourself the stress of trying to do two things at once, and you'd show your friend you cared enough to be there, in mind as well as body.

When a youngster comes to you with a problem or a drawing he did in school just as you're rushing off to your dentist appointment, resist the temptation to deal with two things at once. Tell him you'd like to talk about the problem or look at the picture when you get back and have time to give it your full attention. Even when kids don't have a problem to mull over or something precious to show you, they may just want to shoot the breeze about topics that seem trivial to you—the words to a new record, a progress report on a friend's romance, or a sticker seen in a card shop.

This isn't a major communication event. She won't be offended if you go on feeding the dog or cleaning your carburetor. But how • would you respond if this were an adult friend? You'd probably stop long enough to take in what she says, you'd look at her, and you'd respond in a way that lets her know you heard her. A response like this takes no longer, it helps preserve your peace of mind, and it says, "I care about you."

A Time for Us

If you are as busy as most families these days, spending time together isn't something you can leave to chance. Even your best-meant plans may be derailed by the demands of school, work, and social activities. But if you make it clear that your time together is a top priority, the difficulties can usually be overcome and special times set aside.

Like dinnertime, for example. I know this isn't always easy. Between the kids' activities and your own crowded schedule, you're often lucky if everyone eats, let alone together. If your child has an eating disorder, dinnertime may be an especially trying episode in your day. She may feel uncomfortable about eating with the family, or may cut up your carefully prepared meal into tiny bits to be thrown down the disposal. That's not an easy sight to sit and watch without saying something.

But dinnertime is not the time to say it. As we've seen, you can't possibly come out a winner in the food wars. Be kind to yourself and to her. If she's in treatment, let her therapist deal with the eating problems. Think of the dinner table as a place to talk *with*, not *at* your children.

A useful plan for families whose dinner hours have turned into lectures or gobble-and-run affairs is to set aside one or two evenings a week for family dinners. Everyone must be there. That's the bottom line. No excuse for meetings, dates, or basketball practice. Use this time together to talk about subjects of interest to everyone—like future vacations, movies, what's happening in school.

Some families find that the table talk at their special dinner goes better when they set an agenda. This isn't anything like what goes on in the boardroom at General Motors. It's relaxed and informal. Everyone takes turns deciding what they'd like to talk about. The kids might talk about what they want to do when they grow up, or discuss a pet they'd like to own. They might plan an activity in which one family member would like the others to take part, such as ice-skating lessons, a concert, or a home remodeling project.

After dinner, the family might do something together on a regular basis. Go to a movie or rent a videotape. Take a ride on a bike trail. Play a board game or watch a special television show.

If your daughter has reached an advanced stage of her eating disorder and doesn't want to come to the dinner table at all, you won't gain anything by forcing her. But you can still arrange for times when the whole family can be together.

In one busy family, the parents and their teenaged son and daughter barely see each other all week, but they get together Sunday evenings for "coffee." It's a time when they just relax, have a soda, make popcorn, and find out what everybody's up to. These Sunday evening coffees have become a family tradition that the kids and parents look forward to. It gives everyone the sense of a solid home base, though they're on the wing most of the time.

Families can create their own traditions and rituals for making themselves available to one another. One divorced father fixes his own special brand of Swedish pancakes for their leisurely Sunday breakfast. Then everybody works the Sunday crossword puzzle and heads for a late church service. That's their time together. It's not much, but it's enough to remind them that they're a family.

A Message They Can't Miss

Hugging and touching don't come easy in every family. If there were unspoken taboos against open displays of affection in your own childhood, the very thought may make you squirm. But it's not a taboo you want to pass on to your kids, is it?

A complaint I hear from many teenaged girls is that their fathers stopped showing them any physical affection after they were 12 or so—no hugging, no physical contact at all. These fathers may feel that it's wrong or inappropriate for them to be openly affectionate with a daughter who is growing into a woman, but it feels like rejection to her. It's a serious blow to her self-esteem.

A father can show physical affection for his daughter in any way that feels natural to him. One 16-year-old patient told me how her father helped her handle the heartbreak of a broken relationship just by sitting down next to her and putting his arm around her shoulders. He didn't say a word. He was speaking the language of the heart, and she understood.

Touching and hugging are easy and painless ways to meet their needs and yours at the same time. Everyone loves a sincere hug—a fact that's made Leo Buscaglia rich and famous. It may not make you famous, but it will make your family life richer. Don't worry if you can't be as flamboyant as Buscaglia: the message will get through.

Touching is a form of feedback. It says clearly, I like you. You're dear to me. I wish you well. You know that's how you feel about your children—most of the time, anyway. But unless they're blessed with ESP, they need you to say so in a way they can't miss.

If you've done any public speaking, you know how often a message you thought was perfectly obvious went right over the heads of your audience because you didn't emphasize it enough. You took it for granted they knew what was in your mind. You couldn't imagine how anyone could miss such a clear and simple idea.

But it happens all the time, especially in family communication. You know that you value your children's health and happiness, but you need to say so—clearly and repeatedly. You know that you'll still like them even if they do things that are unacceptable to the family, but they may not know it. They need to hear it from you.

This message may be easier for you to get across when you realize that they'll like you even when you do unacceptable things. Teenagers are looking for real people in their search for models, not saints and superpeople. Any kind of pretense will stifle the free exchange of feelings you all need. So you have a short fuse; you don't always act the way you think "mature" adults should act. Your children can handle it—if you will erase the perfect parent from your mind and just be yourself.

You're Their Best Teacher

Chris, a 17-year-old patient, recently showed up for her appointment in such a gloomy state she could barely drag herself through the door. She had lost the election for senior class president, an office she'd campaigned hard for and wanted desperately. She was emotionally demolished and felt that life was no longer worth living.

Apparently, no one had ever sat down with this intelligent young woman and explained to her that life is a mixed bag, that we win some and lose some. Chris had the impression that losing the election was an unnaturally cruel event, rather than a part of life's normal ups and downs. She felt not only disappointed but diminished as a person.

This talk of life as a mixture of sunshine and shadow is obvious to most adults and may sound trite. But your kids weren't born knowing facts like these. They need to learn them so they won't be devastated every time the wheel of fortune turns. And you are the best teacher.

Let your children in on your own feelings about events that are happening in your life now and those that happened in the past. If you miss out on a promotion or lose your job or your spouse, show them that you're deeply disappointed but no less of a person. Let them see that it's not the end of the world.

If you and your spouse quarrel, a polite cover-up won't help the kids resolve conflicts of their own. And if marital conflict gets to be a way of life, seek help. In this way, your children can see how you solve the kinds of problems they're likely to encounter at some point in their own lives. They can see for themselves that problems make us stronger when we confront them squarely.

Did a steady date in high school ditch you? Tell the kids about it. Let them know how you felt when you were always the last one picked for the team. They need to know that you had many of the same feelings and experiences they do, and they want to know how you handled them.

Parents are often reluctant to share their disappointments and conflicts with children. Part of their reason, I think, is that they'd like to protect them from trouble and sadness. But part of our reluctance to share the darker side of life with kids goes back once again to the perfect-parent myth. Perfect parents never even feel disappointment or anger—they rise above it. But perfect parents, if they existed, couldn't teach their kids a thing about how to live.

Building Bridges and Opening Doors

When Allison got a small part in her school's performance of *West Side Story*, she didn't really expect her mother to attend. She knew that her mother, a counselor at the county detention center, was scheduled to work nights that week. Allison assured her mother she didn't mind, it was only a tiny part, and she wasn't especially good anyhow. But Allison's mother arranged to have her work assignment changed, saying "I don't care how good you are. You took all that time rehearsing, and I'd just like to be there with you that night."

Though Allison acted unconcerned about whether anyone showed up or not, she was pleased that her mother made the effort to be there, as well as relieved that her mother didn't expect her to be the star of the show. This last point is important. If your kids are involved in drama, dance, music, or sports, they want you to be involved and interested in their activities—up to a point. Too much emphasis on their achievements in these areas may make them feel that you're more interested in their high scores and accomplishments than you are in them. This pressure to win can turn an enjoyable activity into a source of anxiety for them.

But if you attend their events for the sake of sharing these experiences with them, they'll know and appreciate the fact that their world is real for you, too. They'll understand that you don't have unspoken expectations and that you don't want to control their lives. They'll welcome your interest.

Another way to show children that their world is real for you is to develop a memory for details. Remember the names of their teachers, their friends, and their favorite rock groups. When a child tells you about a funny or scary event in her life, let it register. Remember the people involved and where it took place, even though it may not seem earthshaking to you.

In fact, many of your child's interests may not seem very exciting or even agreeable to you. But in that case, she'll appreciate your involvement all the more. One of my happiest childhood memories is of my mother sharing my early enthusiasm for snakes—helping me find library books about them, even letting me keep one in my room though they gave her the creeps. Her desire to share my interest helped build a bridge between my world and hers.

You can build bridges between their world and your work away from home. One mother went to the trouble to have a print that her daughter made in graphic arts class beautifully framed and hung in her outer office where all her clients could enjoy it. A schoolteacher father often asks his son to product-test classroom games before he springs them on his junior-high math students.

Respect Their Privacy

While you're getting involved in their lives, it's also important to remember that there will be times, events, and feelings they may not want to share. You will want to wait for an invitation, spoken or sensed, to enter and get involved in their world. If you assume it's your duty as a parent to know what your kids are thinking and feeling at all times, you may have the door slammed in your face.

This is what happened to Darcy's mother. She called me in tears not long ago to say that Darcy, who'd always greeted her when she got home from work, had for the past week taken to staying in her room with the door shut. Always before, Darcy had sat down at the kitchen table with her while she had a soda and talked about her day. Now, she said, she felt that she'd done something to make her daughter angry, that she didn't like her, and that she'd failed as a mother.

What I tried to explain to her was that Darcy was beginning to feel the need for privacy, and that it was no reflection on her as a mother. Darcy was uncomfortable with the degree of closeness, the kind of schoolgirl companionship, that her mother was asking of her.

Trying to play too great a part in their social life or activities may make kids close the door, too. If they're involved in sports, they won't welcome too many questions about their training schedule. They may not want to share all the details of what happened on a date or at a party, and may question your motives for wanting to know.

Needless to say, intrusive tactics like listening in on telephone calls or opening a child's mail are best left to the CIA. And most kids resent parents who straighten out their dresser drawers or rearrange their closets. Too great and obvious a desire not just to share but to manage and oversee a child's life can only create mistrust and make it impossible to open that door to free communication.

They're One of a Kind

Did you ever know someone who knew exactly how to choose the right kind of gift, one that seemed to make you more aware of your own individuality? My father was like that. As a kid, I wasn't very good in sports, but I did get interested in fishing as a young teenager. Though I never said much about it, my dad picked up on my new interest. Every time he went on a trip out of town, he'd bring me back a new fishing lure. It was just a small, inexpensive gift, but I knew my dad was busy and had taken the time to go pick it out just for me. It made me feel good, not only about him but about myself.

We all like this kind of validation of ourselves and our special quirks and interests. A youngster whose favorite color is purple will feel much more of a special person if you bring home the beautiful purple hyacinth you found in the supermarket, or a purple mechanical pencil or hair clip. It doesn't have to be costly, and it doesn't have to be for any special occasion. Much better if it isn't, in fact. Too often we get the feeling that special-occasion gifts are bought out of a sense of obligation.

It's Okay to Make Mistakes

It's important to let kids know—especially if they tend to be perfectionists—that mistakes are natural and acceptable. They often believe, deep down, that they'll be rejected as no-good, worthless people if they make a mistake. If this is how they feel, they certainly won't come and talk to you when they get into any kind of trouble.

One way to get across the message that mistakes are okay is by admitting honestly to your own mistakes, without calling yourself stupid or blaming someone else. We all know people who find somebody to blame—parents, spouse, the government, the weather—whenever anything goes wrong in their life.

"It wasn't my fault I got a speeding ticket. I told you to get the speedometer fixed!" "You'd drink too, if you put up with the pressures I have at work." Putting the blame somewhere else teaches kids that it's not okay to be imperfect. What they need is to hear you come out and say, "I screwed up, but I'm doing things differently now."

The way you handle their mistakes is important, too. What would happen if you noticed a nasty dent in the door of your brand-new Buick, and your daughter admitted she was responsible? Would you go up in smoke, so that she'd resolve never again to tell the truth? Or would you give her credit for her honesty and show her that she and her feelings are more important to you than a hunk of mechanized metal? If she dented the car through recklessness, you'd need to remind her firmly of her responsibilities as a driver, but it could be done lovingly. You shouldn't discourage her from telling you the things you need to know.

Stress the Positive

Another way to let your children know you care about them, and to help them like themselves more, too, is to take every opportunity to notice their strengths. It's an easy habit for any family to form—looking for the good qualities in one another and expressing appreciation.

I sometimes suggest that family members get together occasionally and take turns expressing all the nonphysical things they like about themselves. Try it sometime. It's surprisingly hard for many people to do, but it's good practice in helping members of the family see the positive qualities in each other and in themselves.

Another good exercise is asking each family member in turn to draw up a "celebration list" of all their successes in the past year. These successes shouldn't be limited to the big things that impressed the boss, the teacher, or the neighbors, but should include small personal triumphs. Like the time you were assertive with the telephone company, or installed a garage-door opener without breaking any bones, or gave a five-minute talk for the 4H Club.

We tend to think everybody else is doing things better than we are because we know our shortcomings better than we know anyone else's. Our imperfections make it difficult for us to recognize and appreciate our successes. You know how nervous you were when you made that complaint about your telephone service. You know it took a lot longer to install that door-opener than it "should have." Your daughter knows she left some points out of her talk and that she was shaking in her shoes the whole time. And, since all we see of other people is their exterior, we forget that everybody else is fumbling around feeling scared and insecure, too.

By learning to appreciate and enjoy your own daily successes, you'll also appreciate your child's successes more. You can help her feel that she doesn't have to get an Olympic gold medal to feel like a winner.

It's Not too Late

Beth was very upset the first time she talked to me. Communication in her family had broken down almost completely, she said. Her daughter Tina was spending nearly all her time either in her room or out running. She had withdrawn from her parents and even from her younger sister. There were daily fights at breakfast and dinner, and the stress was begining to affect Beth's relationship with her husband.

"I'm afraid things have gone too far," she said. "We never did talk together very much, and now I don't know where to start. How can we help Tina?"

Like many, Tina's parents found themselves at an impasse as Tina's eating disorder went from bad to worse. They loved their children. They'd always related to them as "perfect parents," kind and all-knowing. That didn't seem to be working any more, though. They had never talked with Tina about her feelings, preferring to discuss school, sports, and her physical needs. Now, they didn't know one another very well. They needed to establish intimacy and trust with their daughter.

I suggested to Beth that she first talk with her husband, then sit down with the whole family. She might say, "I know we've never talked together much before, but we'd like to start doing it more now. We're a family. We care about one another. Can we think of ways we could get to know each other better?"

Knowing one another better means sharing things about ourselves that matter. It means coming out of hiding and discussing feelings and experiences that don't necessarily fit the perfect-parent image. It means revealing the "me" behind the mask. This kind of sharing doesn't come easy, and it doesn't come overnight.

Many of the exercises and activities I suggest to families may seem corny and contrived at first. I suggest activities like sharing your happiest memory, your dreams for the future, the things you most like in other people. You can make up your own topics, or you can buy a commercial game to help you out. It's called The Ungame, made by the Ungame Company in Anaheim, California. It's available in most toy and hobby stores. In this game, participants share their views on questions like "give an example of heaven on earth," "what do you think about when you can't fall asleep," and "describe a happy family." The ground rules allow no talking while others are speaking or laughing to cover up embarrassment— valuable real-life skills.

Exactly what you decide to do to improve family communication is less important than the desire to do it. The simple desire conveys a message of caring to the children. And asking for their help will go a long way toward breaking down any resistance they might have about making changes in the family.

I constantly remind parents that good family communication doesn't just happen. It's a set of habits and attitudes that anyone who wants to can learn. It just takes some time and attention.

It may take written reminders (Have you hugged a child today?); it may take professional help. However, by laying the groundwork—letting your child know she belongs to a caring family, one that feels good to be a part of—you can help her recover from an eating disorder. Or prevent her from ever developing one.

AUTHOR'S NOTE

We have covered a lot of ground together, and I applaud you for investing this time and energy toward improving your relationship with your children and family. Reading this book can help you prevent an eating disorder or help your child with an eating disorder make healthy changes in her life.

But reading a book is only the first step. A philosopher once said, "To know and not to do is really not to know." So I want to encourage you to reread sections of this book that you found helpful. Then incorporate this knowledge into your life so that positive change can take place. And please remember, prevention starts with you.

Appendix 1

Anorexia nervosa. An eating disorder characterized by a loss of 15 percent or more of original body weight and a refusal to maintain a weight considered normal for the person's age and height; intense fear of gaining weight or becoming fat, even though underweight; a distorted body image; and loss of menstrual cycle. Although the term *anorexia* means "loss of appetite," actual loss of appetite is rare among victims of *anorexia nervosa.*

Medical complications: dry, brittle, thinning hair; constipation; lowering of inner body temperature; malnutrition; dehydration; heart palpitations; brain starvation, causing disorganized thinking, concentration problems, misperceptions of the environment; interruption of the menstrual cycle; hormone imbalances; low sodium and potassium levels; atrophy of reproductive organs (in severe, long-term anorexia); osteoporosis; lowered blood pressure; death in 10 percent of cases.

Bulimarexia. A term coined by two clinicians, Marlene Boskind-White and William C. White. Refers to the habitual behavior of gorging and purging, with dynamics that include perfectionism, obsessive concern with food and body proportions, low self-esteem, and a strong commitment to pleasing others. This term is not recognized by most clinicians and researchers in the eating disorders field.

Bulimia nervosa. An eating disorder characterized by recurrent episodes of binge eating; the sense of a lack of control over eating behavior; self-induced vomiting; use of laxatives or diuretics; strict dieting or fasting; vigorous exercising; persistent excessive concern with body shape and weight. Body weight is usually normal.

Medical complications: dehydration; electrolyte imbalances; low sodium and potassium levels; liver damage; kidney damage; severe dental complications from vomiting; constipation; salivary-gland inflammation and

167

swelling (a "chipmunk face"); severe bowel abnormalities; internal bleeding from vomiting; stomach ulcers; lacerations or ulcers of the esophagus from vomiting; heart palpitations; heart attack; death in severe cases.

Diuretic abuse. A practice by some patients with eating disorders. Diuretics rid the body of fluid, which is replaced as soon as their use is stopped. Diuretics can upset the body's normal mineral balance, leading to a dangerous loss of sodium and potassium. They may cause dizziness, weakness, and nausea.

Electrolyte imbalance. Electrolytes are the charged particles in each cell of the body that stimulate muscles to function. When an imbalance occurs, as from purging or laxative, diuretic, or ipecac abuse, the person may experience muscle cramping or heartbeat irregularities. In severe cases, the muscles stop working and heart attack may occur.

"Fear" foods. Any food that creates tension, anxiety, or fear for the eating-disorder sufferer. Usually a food of high calorie or fat content.

Hyperalimentation. To give rapid nourishment. May be used with severely anorexic patients in the form of intravenous feeding.

Intensive outpatient program. Typically a day or evening program, consisting mainly of group therapy, that the patient attends for three to four hours each day, three to five times a week. The length of the program varies from four to twelve weeks. By the end of the program, the patient attends only once a week.

Patients may be referred to an intensive outpatient program under these conditions: (1) The case isn't severe enough for inpatient care but requires more structure than the typical outpatient program provides; (2) The program may be part of a total eating-disorders program, following hospitalization and preceding the less structured outpatient program; (3) The insurance company may stipulate that the person try intensive outpatient care before agreeing to cover costs of inpatient care.

Ipecac abuse. Ipecac is a poison that the body rejects, causing vomiting. Usually given to children who have swallowed poison, ipecac is used by some bulimics to induce vomiting after eating. Abuse of ipecac is deadly. It builds up in the body and causes electrolyte imbalance and sodium and potassium imbalance, conditions that can result in death.

Outpatient therapy. A clinic or private practice in which the therapist specializes in treating eating disorders. Treatment typically involves individual, family, and/or group therapy. Dietary, occupational, and recreational therapy are often available. Psychological testing may be offered. An after-care phase of treatment is usually available.

Relapse. A "slip backward" into the eating-disorder behavior or thinking that may occur after progress has been made in treatment. Relapse is often viewed as negative and to be avoided. It is, however, a positive sign, showing that the patient is at a point in her treatment where she is trying something new. It is a learning experience and a sign of progress.

Restricting. Cutting back on food intake as practiced by victims of anorexia nervosa or bulimia nervosa. May mean restricting the amount eaten at each meal or going without food for a day or more. Also refers to a restriction of calories after a "fear food" is eaten.

Sodium- and potassium-level imbalance. Sodium and potassium are part of the complex system that enables each cell of the body to function through electrical stimulation. Sodium and potassium levels may be dangerously reduced as a result of frequent vomiting or abuse of laxatives, diuretics, or syrup of ipecac. When this happens, the cells do not function properly. The result may be muscle cramping, heartbeat irregularities, and, in extreme cases, death.

APPENDIX 2

Four Major Approaches to Eating Disorders Therapy

The *psychodynamic approach* to therapy focuses on the past, particularly on how childhood events affect the person's present functioning. The goal is to uncover unconscious areas of conflict and bring them to conscious awareness so that they can be dealt with constructively.

According to psychodynamic theory, the forces within the mind are in continual conflict with one another, creating anxiety that the individual deals with in a variety of unhealthy ways. Unacceptable impulses may be pushed into the unconscious and repressed. Internal threats may be transformed into external threats by a process called *projection*. Painful feelings may be denied, or they may be avoided by intellectualizing about them.

Psychodynamic therapy is based on the assumption that these buried thoughts and feelings can be brought into consciousness, but only under special circumstances. Dreams, for example, provide important insights. Unconscious thoughts and feelings can also be constructed in the course of the therapy sessions. A major component of this kind of therapy is the forming of an ambiguous but dependable relationship with the therapist and an analysis by the therapist and patient of what this relationship means to the patient. The purpose of this work is to help the patient form satisfactory relationships outside the therapy and to develop realistic goals.

Many psychologists today criticize the psychodynamic approach as unscientific. The theories of Freud, on which this approach to therapy is based, can't be tested; they are supported only by case studies rather than large-scale scientific research. Moreover, these case studies are drawn from a limited sample of middle-class patients. Another strong objection to this approach is its pessimism. It views human beings as nearly helpless to change themselves after events in the first six years of life have taken their toll. Finally, psychodynamic therapy is notoriously time-consuming and expensive.

But even its critics concede that psychodynamic therapy can help patients gain greater mastery of their behavior by forcing them to confront and understand their unconscious impulses. Despite its drawbacks, it works very well for some people.

The *cognitive-behavioral approach* is based on the belief that emotional problems result from faulty thinking and distorted attitudes toward the self and others. Unlike psychodynamic therapy, the focus here is on present thought processes. The patient's behavior is usually seen as a learned adaptation to a conflict, and the goal of the therapy is to help patients unlearn these adaptations and change their thinking. In therapy of eating disorders, the patient's belief system, as well as her thoughts and images, need to be changed.

Because change is seen as a learning process, behavioral theorists, such as B. F. Skinner, have focused on the ways in which learning takes place. Some mechanisms of learning that play an important part in behavioral theory are *generalization, discrimination, reinforcement,* and *modeling.*

An individual who has been conditioned to respond to a particular stimulus in a certain way may learn to respond to similar stimuli in the same way by the process of *generalization.* For example, a young woman whose boyfriend has told her she is too fat may come to believe that every man will think she is too fat. Through the process of *discrimination,* the person can learn to limit the effects of generalization by distinguishing among similar stimuli and responding only to those that are appropriate. Instead of believing every man will think she is too fat because her boyfriend thinks so, the young woman can learn to remind herself of the men she knows who don't consider her too fat.

Reinforcement is a particularly powerful means of promoting or eliminating behaviors. The dieter who is praised for losing weight is being reinforced in her behavior and motivated to continue dieting. An undesirable behavior can be eliminated by discovering what is reinforcing it and removing the reinforcement. *Modeling* is a means of learning by being rewarded for an imitative response. A father teaching his son to lift weights would probably demonstrate the correct techniques and reward the boy with praise if he imitated them, motivating him to continue lifting weights.

Cognitive-behavioral therapists use a variety of techniques to correct the patient's erroneous views and change her behavior. She may be asked to keep records of desirable and undesirable thoughts and the circumstances in which they occurred. She may visualize how she will feel and act when the new ways of thinking are established. She will reinforce her new thinking by controlled practice in the real world, until the new way of thought becomes habitual. In the process, the patient learns specific skills that are directly related to her present problem. These may include relaxation training, anxiety management, and problem solving. The final objective is to increase the patient's coping ability and her sense of competence.

The main criticism of cognitive-behavioral therapy is that many of its principles evolved from experiments with animals, and some psychologists question whether such principles are fully applicable to human beings. They feel that the behaviorists' reduction of behavior to measurable units oversimplifies human experience. On the other hand, behavioral therapy has produced promising results. It is also less expensive and time-consuming than most other forms of treatment.

The *humanistic approach* to therapy was developed during the 1940s and 1950s by Abraham Maslow, Carl Rogers, and other psychologists who thought therapy focused too much on mental illness and too little on the individual's well-being and potential for growth. A common assumption of humanistic therapy is that emotional problems are caused by the "shoulds" and "oughts" on which many individuals base their belief system. The main goal of the therapist is to provide an environment in which self-cure can take place by helping patients eliminate the "shoulds" and connect with the true inner self.

Humanistic therapy is similar to psychodynamic therapy in that both regard abnormal behavior as resulting from anxiety when part of the self is denied. The goal of therapy in both approaches is to elicit insights that will help patients reclaim that lost part of the self. But in psychodynamic therapy the insights are provided mainly by the therapist, based on interpretations of repressed thoughts and feelings from the patient's past. In humanistic therapy, on the other hand, the insights come from the patients themselves as they explore thoughts and feelings about their *present* life. A major difference between the two approaches is that psychodynamic therapists judge behavior as normal or abnormal based on cultural norms; humanistic therapists believe individuals are capable of judging for themselves whether their behavior needs to be changed, without reference to their social adjustment.

Like cognitive-behavior therapy, the humanistic approach sees faulty learning as the source of emotional problems. A crucial difference is that cognitive-behavioral therapists believe human behavior is determined by conditioning and changed by stimuli that elicit new responses. They reject as unscientific the humanistic therapists' belief in personal insight as the main tool of therapy. Whether or not this humanistic faith in individual judgment can be justified, it does enhance patients' self-esteem and has encouraged many to make constructive changes in their behavior.

The *addictions approach* is based on the assumption that an eating disorder or alcohol or drug abuse is an illness over which the individual has little or no control. Patients learn that their behavior can be stopped only by abstaining from the abuse substance, whether it is alcohol or refined sugar. The spiritual needs of the patient are emphasized, along with the concept of group support. Treatment is frequently provided by people who were addicted and are now in recovery.

This approach is frequently called the twelve-step model. First developed by Alcoholics Anonymous, the twelve steps have been adapted and used as a program of recovery by other programs, such as Overeaters Anonymous. The steps[1] are as follows:

1. We admitted that we were powerless over food and that our lives had become unmanageable.
2. We came to believe that a Power greater than ourselves could restore us to sanity.
3. We made a decision to turn our will and our lives over to the care of God as we understood Him.
4. We made a searching and fearless moral inventory of ourselves.
5. We admitted to God, to ourselves, and to another human being the exact nature of our wrongs.
6. We were entirely ready to have God remove all these defects of character.
7. We humbly asked Him to remove our shortcomings.
8. We made a list of all persons we had harmed, and became willing to make amends to them all.
9. We made direct amends to such people wherever possible, except when to do so would injure them or others.
10. We continued to take personal inventory and when we were wrong promptly admitted it.
11. We sought through prayer and meditation to improve our conscious contact with God as we understood Him, praying only for knowledge of His will for us and the power to carry that out.
12. Having had a spiritual awakening as the result of these steps, we tried to carry this message to other compulsive overeaters, and to practice these principles in all our affairs.

A disadvantage of twelve-step therapy is that it does not consider stages in the individual's recovery process. The participant is told to avoid "fear foods" at all costs. A binge means she has failed and must start the recovery process over again. A group like Overeaters Anonymous may also encourage participants to identify themselves as "bulimics" or "anorexics" instead of trying to create healthy new identities for themselves.

The major advantage of twelve-step therapy is the strong ongoing group support. In addition, the reliance on a higher power adds a spiritual dimension, lacking in most forms of therapy, that can relieve patients' guilt and promote emotional growth.

Notes

1. *Alcoholics Anonymous*, 3rd. ed., rev. (New York: Alcoholics Anonymous World Services, 1976).

APPENDIX 3

Resources: Eating Disorders Associations and Hospital-Related Programs

Eating Disorders Associations

These nonprofit organizations provide a variety of services to sufferers of eating disorders, their families, and health-care professionals. Services include referral lists, newsletters, and printed information on eating disorders. Some sponsor self-help groups, conferences, and general meetings.

Most of their services are free, and membership dues are modest. When writing to these organizations for information, it's a good idea to include a stamped, self-addressed envelope.

American Anorexia/Bulimia Association, Inc. (AA/BA)
133 Cedar Lane
Teaneck, NY 07666
(201) 836-1800

Anorexia Nervosa and Related Eating Disorders, Inc. (ANRED)
P.O. Box 5102
Eugene, OR 97405
(503) 344-1144

175

National Anorexic Aid Society, Inc. (NAAS)
550 South Cleveland Avenue, Suite F
Westerville, OH 43081
(614) 436-1112

National Association of Anorexia Nervosa and Associated Disorders,
    Inc. (ANAD)
P.O. Box 271
Highland Park, IL 60035
(312) 831-3438

Hospital-Related Programs

California

Eating Disorders Program
Glendale Adventist Medical Center
1509 Wilson Terrace
Glendale, CA 91206
(818) 409-8280

Children's Hospital at Stanford
520 Sand Hill Road
Palo Alto, CA 94304
(415) 327-4800

Eating Disorders Program
Neuropsychiatric Institute
University of California at Los Angeles
760 Westwood Plaza
Los Angeles, CA 90024-1759
(213) 825-0491

St. Helena Hospital and Health Center
610 Sanitarium Road
Deer Park, CA 94576
(707) 963-6361

Colorado

Eating Disorders Program
Memorial Hospital, Boulder
311 Mapleton Avenue
Boulder, CO 80302
(303) 441-0560
Outpatient:
Fort Collins Eating Disorders Program
419 Canyon Avenue, Suite 310
Fort Collins, CO 80521
(303) 484-6913

Eating Disorders Program
Porter Memorial Hospital
2525 South Downing Street
Denver, CO 80210
(303) 778-5831

District of Columbia

Children's Hospital—National Medical Center
Department of Psychiatry
111 Michigan Avenue
Washington, D.C., 20010
(202) 754-5386 (information)

Georgia

Eating Disorders Program
Smyrna Hospital
3949 South Cobb Drive
Smyrna, GA 30081
(404) 432-2188

Illinois

Eating Disorders Research and Treatment Program
Department of Psychiatry
Michael Reese Hospital and Medical Center
Lake Shore Drive at 31st Street
Chicago, IL 60616
(312) 791-3878

Eating Disorders Program
Northwestern Memorial Hospital
320 East Huron
Chicago, IL 60611
(312) 908-7850

Maryland

Eating and Weight Disorders Clinic
Johns Hopkins Medical Institutions
Meyer Building 3-181
600 North Wolfe Street
Baltimore, MD 21205
(301) 955-3863

Massachusetts

Anorexia Nervosa and Associated Disorders Clinic
Children's Hospital Medical Center
Department of Psychiatry
300 Longwood Avenue
Boston, MA 02115
(617) 735-6728

Eating Disorders Unit
Massachusetts General Hospital
15 Parkman Street
Boston, MA 02114
(617) 726-2724

Minnesota

Eating Disorders Clinic
University of Minnesota Hospital and Clinic
420 Delaware Street S.E.
Box 301 Mayo
Minneapolis, MN 55455
(612) 626-6188, (612) 626-3463

Missouri

Anorexia/Bulimia Treatment and Education Center
St. John's Mercy Medical Center
615 South New Ballas Road
St. Louis, MO 63141
(314) 569-6898

New York

Eating Disorders Program
New York Hospital
Cornell University Medical Center
21 Bloomingdale Road
White Plains, NY 10605
(914) 682-9100

Ohio

Cleveland Clinic Foundation
Section of Child and Adolescent Psychiatry
9500 Euclid Avenue
Cleveland, OH 44106
(216) 444-5812

Center for Eating Disorders Clinic
University of Cincinnati College of Medicine
Department of Psychiatry
231 Bethesda Avenue
Cincinnati, OH 45267
(513) 872-5118

Oregon

Eating Disorders Program
Portland Adventist Medical Center
10123 Southeast Market Street
Portland, OR 97216
(503) 251-6101

Eating Disorders Treatment Program
Sacred Heart General Hospital in cooperation with Anorexia Nervosa
 and Related Eating Disorders, Inc.
P.O. Box 10905
Eugene, OR 97440
(503) 686-7372

Pennsylvania

Philadelphia Child Guidance Clinic
Two Children's Center
34th Street and Civic Center Boulevard
Philadelphia, PA 19104
(215) 243-2830

South Carolina

Eating Disorders Program
St. Francis Hospital
One Francis Drive
Greenville, SC 29601
(803) 255-1842

Tennessee

Eating Disorders Program
Tennessee Christian Medical Center
500 Hospital Drive
Madison, TN 37115
(615) 865-3201

Texas

Eating Disorders Program
Huguley Memorial Medical Center
11801 South Freeway
Fort Worth, TX 76115
(817) 551-2788

Washington

Eating Disorders Program
Saint Cabrini Hospital
Terry and Madison
Seattle, WA 98104
(206) 621-3700

Wisconsin

Center for Eating Disorders
30 South Henry Street
Madison, WI 53708
(608) 258-3270

Jackson Clinic
345 West Washington Avenue
Madison, WI 53703
(608) 252-8661

SUGGESTED READING

Eating Disorders and Weight Consciousness

Bruch, Hilde. *The Golden Cage: The Enigma of Anorexia Nervosa*. Cambridge, MA: Harvard University Press, 1978.

Cauwels, Janice M. *Bulimia—The Binge-Purge Compulsion*. Garden City, NY: Doubleday, 1983.

Chernin, Kim. *The Obsession: Reflections on the Tyranny of Slenderness*. New York: Harper & Row, 1981.

Garfinkel, Paul E. and David M. Garner. *Anorexia Nervosa: A Multidimensional Perspective*. New York: Brunner/Mazel, 1982.

Hollis, Judi. *Fat is a Family Affair*. Center City, MN: Hazelden Foundation, 1985.

Jacobsen, Beverly. *Anorexia Nervosa and Bulimia: Two Severe Eating Disorders*. New York: Public Affairs Committee, 1985. (Pamphlet)

Kinoy, Barbara, Ed. *When Will We Laugh Again?* New York: Columbia University Press, 1984. (On family therapy)

Levenkron, Steven. *The Best Little Girl in the World*. New York: Warner Books, 1979. (Fiction)

———. *Kessa*. New York: Warner Books, 1986. (Fiction, sequel to 1978 book)

———. *Treating and Overcoming Anorexia Nervosa*. New York: Warner Books, Inc., 1983.

Roth, Geneen. *Feeding the Hungry Heart: The Experience of Compulsive Eating*. New York: Bobbs-Merrill, 1982.

Ruckman, Ivy. *The Hunger Scream*. New York: Walker and Company, 1983. (Fiction)

Sandbek, Terence J., Ph.D. *The Deadly Diet: Recovering From Anorexia and Bulimia*. Oakland, CA: New Harbinger, 1986.

Squire, Susan. "Why Thousands of Women Don't Know How to Eat Normally Anymore." *Glamour*, October 1981.

———. *The Slender Balance*. New York: G. P. Putnam's Sons, 1983.

183

Self-Help

Alberti, Robert E., and Michael L. Emmons. *Your Perfect Right: A Guide to Assertive Living*, 5th ed. San Ramon, CA: Impact Publications, 1986.

Burns, David. *Feeling Good*. New York: William Morrow, 1980.

Dyer, Wayne. *Pulling Your Own Strings*. New York: Avon Books, 1979.

———. *Your Erroneous Zones*. New York: Avon Books, 1976.

Freed, Alvyn M. *TA for Teens*. Rolling Hills Estate, CA: Jalmer Press, 1976.

Gardner-Loulan, JoAnn et al. *Period*. San Francisco: Volcano Press, 1979. (Advice for young girls on menstruation)

Hutchinson, Marcia G. *Transforming Body Image: Learning to Love the Body You Have*. Trumansburg, NY: The Crossing Press, 1985.

Kano, Susan. *Making Peace With Food*. Danbury, CT: Amity Publishing, 1985.

Roth, Geneen. *Breaking Free From Compulsive Eating*. New York: Bobbs-Merrill, 1985.

Schuller, Robert. *You Can Become the Person You Want to Be*. New York: E. P. Dutton, 1973.

Family Interaction

Berne, Pat and Louis M. Savary. *Building Self-Esteem in Children*. New York: Crossroad Publishing, 1985.

Elkind, David. *The Hurried Child: Growing Up Too Fast Too Soon*. Reading, MA: Addison-Wesley, 1981.

Gordon, Thomas. *Parent Effectiveness Training*. New York: Peter H. Wyden, 1970.

Satir, Virginia. *Peoplemaking*. Palo Alto, CA: Science and Behavior Books, 1972.

Nutrition and Health

Aronson, Virginia. *Thirty Days to Better Nutrition*. Garden City: NY: Doubleday, 1984.

Bennett, William and Joel Gurin. *The Dieter's Dilemma*. New York: Basic Books, 1983. (Setpoint theory)

Brody, Jane. *Jane Brody's Good Food Book: Living the High Carbohydrate Way*. New York: W. W. Norton, 1985.

Satter, Ellyn. *Child of Mine: Feeding With Love and Good Sense*. Palo Alto, CA: Bull Publishing, 1979.

———. *How to Get Your Kid to Eat . . . But Not Too Much*. Palo Alto, CA: Bull Publishing, 1987.

INDEX